Praise for

EVERYDAY HOCKEY HEROES

"You can never truly know a country until you know the game that defines the people. The U.S. has football, Brazil soccer, India cricket. If you want to know Canada, or if you're Canadian and want to know yourself, *Everyday Hockey Heroes* is for you. In these moving, inspirational, and entertaining stories, Bob McKenzie, the 'Mr. Hockey' of insight and analysis, and sportscaster extraordinaire Jim Lang have found the pulse of Canada—and the beat is as strong and healthy as ever."

Roy MacGregor, bestselling author of
Wayne Gretzky's Ghost and *The Home Team*

"Inspiring. Truly hard to put down. Bob's and Jim's great storytelling abilities prove that hockey is so much more than just a game. Loved it!"

David Chilton, bestselling author of
The Wealthy Barber

"Hockey never ceases to amaze me with the quality of the people in the game. This book is full of hockey champions who will inspire you and show you the true depth of the people in and around this game."

Brian Burke, former NHL executive

"These heartwarming stories illustrate the power hockey has to unite us and inspire us to be the best we can be."

James Duthie, TSN Hockey host

"My friends Bob McKenzie and Jim Lang have a lifetime of stories from covering the great game, and these pages are wonderful evidence of what they've collected over the years. You'll laugh at times, you'll be inspired at times, and you may even cry as well, but through it all you'll know that Canada is hockey and hockey is Canada. It really is *our* game."

Peter Mansbridge

"Compelling accounts of personal strength and the power of hope. *Everyday Hockey Heroes* gives a spotlight to important issues that people are dealing with and exhibits their ability to not only overcome these obstacles but, more important, to try to make positive change in the wake of them."

Sheldon Kennedy, former NHL player and founder
of the Sheldon Kennedy Child Advocacy Centre

"Bob and Jim shed some fantastic light on a coast to coast truth: there are hockey heroes in every rink in Canada. Names like Westlake, St. Denis, Singh, Potvin, and Cunningham are what drive the success and our love of the game. *Everyday Hockey Heroes* reminds us that you don't need to make a million to be a real hockey hero."

Ken Reid, *Sportsnet Central* anchor and author of
Hockey Card Stories 2

"By seeing hockey at the margins, Bob McKenzie and Jim Lang's work shines with a kind of log-cabin storytelling, illuminating the sport's humanity and showing that every path is crooked no matter where you end up in the game."

Dave Bidini, author of *Keon and Me*
and member of Rheostatics

EVERYDAY HOCKEY HEROES

INSPIRING STORIES ON AND OFF THE ICE

BOB McKENZIE
& JIM LANG

Published by Simon & Schuster

NEW YORK   LONDON   TORONTO   SYDNEY   NEW DELHI

SIMON &
SCHUSTER
CANADA

Library and Archives Canada Cataloguing in Publication

Title: Everyday hockey heroes : inspiring stories on and off the ice / Bob McKenzie & Jim Lang.
Names: McKenzie, Bob, author. | Lang, Jim, 1965– author.
Description: Originally published: Toronto : Simon and Schuster, 2018.
Identifiers: Canadiana 20190088206 | ISBN 9781982104856 (softcover)
Subjects: LCSH: Hockey --Canada --Biography. | LCSH: Hockey --Canada.
Classification: LCC GV848.5.A1.M35 2019 | DDC 796.962092/2 --dc23

ISBN 978-1-9821-0485-6 (pbk)
ISBN 978-1-5082-5916-9 (hc)
ISBN 978-1-5082-5917-6 (ebook)

To Jonathan Pitre, the Humboldt Broncos,
and all the everyday hockey heroes out there

Contents

Introduction by Bob McKenzie   ix

Wayne's Road Hockey Warriors *by Wayne Simmonds*   1

All Heart *by Craig Cunningham*   11

The Hockey Sledgehammer *by Greg Westlake*   29

Reaching Out *by Karina Potvin*   45

The Sweet Sounds of Hockey *by Wayne St. Denis*   57

A Boy with a Dream *by Harnarayan Singh*   69

The Trailblazer *by Andi Petrillo*   89

Life as a Blind and Deaf Hockey Fan *by Christian Holmes*   109

Find a Way *by Ben Fanelli*   117

Saving the Game I Love *by Dr. Charles Tator*   137

Fighting the Good Fight *by Hilary Knight*   151

Shifting the Culture *by Brock McGillis*   167

The Quiet Champion *by Kevin Monkman*   179

The Healing Power of Hockey *by Pat Kline*   199

Until the Job Is Done *by Bob McKenzie*   213

Afterword   241

Acknowledgements   249

Photography Credits   255

Introduction

"Who's gonna be the hero?"

If you've ever played hockey, odds are you have heard that line before. On the bench, in the third period, of a tense, taut tie game. Or maybe in those anxious moments just before the beginning of sudden-death overtime.

"Who wants to be the hero?"

When you're asked to put your name on a book titled *Everyday Hockey Heroes*, it does make you pause and think a little about what it takes to be a hero, to be heroic. And what exactly is a hockey hero anyway?

It could be the player who gets the game-winning goal. There are few feelings in the game that rival that incredible rush of energy and excitement. I mean, let's be honest. Who doesn't love a little adulation and adoration, to be put up on a pedestal? To be the hero.

As I got to thinking about heroes and hockey, it struck me that while there may not be many things as exhilarating as scoring the game-winning goal, does that action really qualify as heroic? A truly heroic act should not be so fleeting as a game-winning goal. It should have a deeper meaning or a greater sense of purpose than a random act in a random game.

When I was getting ready to write this introduction in early April 2018, I was pondering just that, trying to figure out the whole hero thing as it applies to hockey and the title of this book. Then I received some inspiration. Not welcome inspiration, mind you. But inspiration nonetheless.

Now, you may or may not immediately recognize April 6, 2018, as a particularly good or bad day in your life, but let me tell you why it was such a sad and tragic one in the hockey world. That morning we woke up to the heartbreaking news Jonathan Pitre had passed away. He was just seventeen.

If you're not familiar with Jonathan Pitre, his story first came to national prominence in Canada in 2014 when the *Ottawa Citizen* wrote a story about a hockey-loving teenager from Russell, Ontario, who had a rare but excruciatingly painful genetic skin condition known as epidermolysis bullosa (EB). Those born with EB, known as "Butterfly Children" because their skin is as fragile as a butterfly's wings, suffer painful blisters all over their bodies. There's currently no cure, and depending on the severity of the condition, EB can be fatal.

The moment we got to know Jonathan Pitre, he became our hero. He loved sports, especially hockey, and his favourite team was the Ottawa Senators, who embraced him as one of their own. He got to be an NHL scout for a day and spent time with the Senators' management and players. He effectively became an adopted member of the team and a truly beloved member of the NHL community.

In 2015, The Sports Network (TSN) produced and aired *The Butterfly Child*, a touching yet difficult-to-watch documentary about Jonathan's battle with EB. His story went viral. The last time I checked, the YouTube video had close to twelve million views. The video—if you haven't seen it, you really should take the time—introduced the world to a very special boy and his mother, Tina Boileau, whose love and unfailing dedication in caring for Jonathan most certainly qualifies her for some form of sainthood, to say nothing of her own heroism. Jonathan was a true inspiration, who, in the face of second-by-second, minute-by-minute suffering, somehow managed to rise above everything and be cheerful and optimistic, a shining light of life. An example in the art of forging ahead no matter the obstacles, he was wise and philosophical, but also funny and warm, and all of that at such a tender age.

"It's always that battle between pain and not," Jonathan said.

He may have been known as the Butterfly Child, but as he so plainly told us, he had "the heart of a warrior." Indeed he did. Every day, just trying to live was a battle for him, but he was still dedicated to a greater cause—raising awareness and funds for EB.

There's your hero. There's heroism.

All of which made the news of his passing so sad, though it was also hard not to allow that Jonathan's suffering was over, and perhaps he had, finally, found some peace.

That was how Friday, April 6, began. There was no way of knowing how wretchedly tragic it would end.

That same Friday, in the late afternoon–early evening hours, on northbound Highway 35 just north of Tisdale, Saskatchewan, the bus carrying the Humboldt Broncos Junior A team of the Saskatchewan Junior Hockey League—heading to Nipawin for game 5 of their league playoff series—and a semi tractor trailer truck travelling westbound collided. The resulting carnage at the prairie highway intersection was unimaginable.

As soon as the news of the crash filtered out that evening, we knew it would be bad. The Royal Canadian Mounted Police indicated fairly early that there were fatalities. As we waited for more details to emerge, we were reminded of December 30, 1986, when four members of the Western Hockey League's Swift Current Broncos died when their bus hit black ice and overturned, and of January 12, 2008, when a van carrying a boys' high school basketball team in

Bathurst, New Brunswick, crashed in wintry road conditions, killing seven students and the wife of the team's head coach. How could this happen again?

Friday night gave way to the wee hours of Saturday morning, and we learned that the Humboldt Broncos' bus crash was even worse than we'd thought. Fourteen of twenty-nine on the bus had perished. Within a week, two more succumbed to their injuries.

So many young lives ended. So many more forever altered.

It's difficult to conceive of a tragedy that could shred the very fabric of Canadian life the way a fatal bus crash of a junior hockey team could. It was an assault, an affront, to the things the Canadian hockey culture holds near and dear. For many Canadians, hockey is a way of life. It's in our hearts, our blood, our soul.

A hockey team is a family.

In Canada's hockey heartland, in Saskatchewan, in places named Humboldt, Nipawin, Estevan, the Battlefords, Weyburn, Melfort, Melville, Kindersley, and Wilcox, the Junior A teams are extensions of the communities. The players could be locals; they could be from far and wide. The owners, the executives, the management, the coaches, the trainers, the players, the billet families, the sponsors, the media, the fans, the townspeople—they are, in a sense, all one.

We in the hockey community are, in that same sense, all one, too, an extended family of sorts, especially when tough times hit, when tragedy strikes and we don't have to squint too hard to see how easily we could be walking in someone else's shoes. For us, there's supposed to be a certain sanctity and safety on a team bus. It's where friendships and families are forged, not where they come to a tragic end. Yet on that fateful night, they did. The pain of the Humboldt tragedy transcended that little prairie community because hockey people—Canadians all across the vast land, in small communities and big cities, and in the NHL and every hockey league below it—know what it's like to have your children on a bus, to chase their hockey dreams. So to see such a special tradition go horribly wrong on such a massive scale, well, no matter how far away from Humboldt you may find yourself, it hits close to home. Hits you hard.

Sleep, or any kind of peace, was difficult to come by that Friday night in April. It's why I lay there awake, tossing and turning, unable to stop thinking of the courageous Jonathan Pitre and the sorrow his mom, Tina, must have been feeling, unable to shake the image of the Humboldt Broncos' bus crash, unable to stop thinking about all those young lives snuffed out and their grief-stricken family members experiencing such incredible loss but still very much alive, left to pick up the pieces of lives forever altered if not shattered.

After I finally did fall asleep for a few hours, I woke up the next morning and started looking for a little perspective and, damn, there it was: the bright light of inspiration among all that darkness.

Hope.

If you allow yourself, it's easy to get overwhelmed by what I sometimes refer to as the "infinite sadness" in life, but that's where our heroes come in—those who in the face of terrible adversity strive for a better life, not just for themselves, but for others, too.

Jonathan Pitre, of course, understood this better than anyone. When asked if he thought about the future and the reality that EB sufferers often don't live past thirty, Jonathan replied that he had, but he pushed it aside.

"Yes, I thought about it for sure," he said. "I mean, how can't you? It's a reality. I'm here. I'm going to go step by step, day by day. You never know what's going to happen. I could live to be one hundred. You can't know. But I know I'm not going to stop anytime soon. I'm going to keep going."

It's amazing to me that at the age of fourteen, Jonathan was as wise as the great philosophers and emperors of ancient Greece and Rome.

I often think of the Latin phrase *memento mori*, which translates to "Remember you must die." Far from being morbid, *memento mori* is the practice of taking the time to reflect on your own mortality so that you live life to the fullest. The great Roman emperor Marcus Aurelius, whose meditations are the foundation of Stoic philosophy, simply put it this way: "You could leave life right now. Let that determine what you do and say and think." Modern-day Stoics say, "Death doesn't make life pointless but rather purposeful."

We see this all the time when tragedy strikes. What starts as darkness, ends as light.

After the initial shock, horror, and grief of the Humboldt Broncos' bus crash came an outpouring of care, generosity, and a truer sense of community. From the first responders, the passersby, and the hospital staff, who did whatever possible to help, to the grief-stricken families, who told the stories of their departed children, paying tribute to their lives, not their deaths, we saw strength and courage everywhere. We tried to do the same, as best we could. In the first week after the accident, upwards of $11 million were earmarked for Humboldt and the Broncos. A simple symbolic gesture of leaving a hockey stick out at the front door and the porch light on—Sticks Out for Humboldt—went viral. From throughout the NHL to the little hamlets across the country and beyond, all these individual acknowledgments created an enormous swell of compassion and hope.

Humboldt Strong.

We Are All Broncos.

There's an old saying from the American novelist James Lane Allen that goes, "Adversity doesn't build character, it reveals it." Many of us in hockey have appropriated that quotation, replacing "adversity" with "hockey."

Hockey doesn't build character, it reveals it. That's at the core of the game, and it's that sentiment that binds the community at its most broken times. Hockey isn't just a game for those who love it, it's the living embodiment of a belief system, a reflection of who we strive to be, on or off the ice, in spite of pain and hardships. The struggle is real. The quest to get there, well, that's absolutely heroic.

Which brings us back to this book in your hands. It is, I firmly believe, a series of stories from people who embody the values and beliefs that are foundational in hockey and have applied them in a much broader sense to be their best selves.

Now, I have to be perfectly honest. When I was first asked if I would be interested in being involved in this project, putting my name to this book and taking on the responsibility that goes with it, I was hesitant. You might even say skeptical. *Everyday Hockey Heroes* is a series of first-person stories. They aren't *my* stories. I didn't write them.

I've written two books: *Hockey Dad: True Confessions of a (Crazy?) Hockey Parent* and *Hockey Confidential: Inside Stories from People Inside the Game*. Both were, for me, deeply personal experiences. Every aspect of them was mine. The first book was all about my family and the trials and tribulations of raising my two sons in the Canadian minor hockey system. The second book was an anthology of stories I've always wanted to tell—stories that I felt transcended hockey and were much more about life than just the "sweaty game," as my dear departed friend Gord Downie would often call it.

I just wasn't sure if or where I might fit in with *Everyday Hockey Heroes*.

Then I read a proposed chapter on Philadelphia Flyer Wayne Simmonds and what it was like for a young black hockey player in Scarborough, Ontario—which happens to be where I grew up—to try to make it in an almost exclusively white game. The story of his family being unable to afford AAA hockey fees and the extraordinary measures Wayne took to play the game was incredibly moving. I was hooked. It's a great story about hockey and an even better story about life.

Then I read the story of Wayne St. Denis, an otherwise normal hockey-loving teenager from Windsor, Ontario, who without warning started losing his eyesight to the point of being declared legally blind. But he found an outlet for his passion to play hockey, blind hockey, with the Toronto Ice Owls and gave a life that had lost much of its meaning renewed vigour.

One of the stories was about a famous NHL player; the other was about a man I'd never heard of. It didn't matter. They both spoke to me. They both inspired me.

The roster of some of the other potential stories in the book was equally motivational: Team Canada sledge hockey captain Greg Westlake, who did not let the amputation of both legs when he was a youngster prevent him from fulfilling his dreams of being a world champion player; Karina Potvin, a high school teacher from Ottawa who is dedicated to teaching hockey and Canadian culture to Syrian refugee children; Harnarayan Singh, a Punjabi broadcaster who worked so hard to make his mark on air as part of *Hockey Night in Canada*; Kevin Monkman, a Manitoba Métis who took his own experiences as a player and paid them forward by being a championship coach whose priority is now developing indigenous players; Pat Kline, a Nova Scotia firefighter, and the ties that bind, hockey and otherwise, him and his late father, Ray; Andi Petrillo, a TV host and the daughter of Italian immigrants, and her journey to break through the male-dominated world of hockey broadcasting; Brock McGillis, whose love of hockey was marred by the fear that his teammates would find out that he was gay, but who found the strength to embrace who he was, becoming the first openly gay professional hockey player; and Christian Holmes, who is inspired by the game to keep fighting the physical barriers in his way.

What I quickly realized was how many inspiring stories are out there, just waiting to be told. Hockey is such a wonderful setting for smart, tough, innovative, caring, and heroic people to show us the way, not just within the game but in life. I knew that if I were going to be involved, I would need, and want, to bring more to the table than just my name.

That part would not be difficult. I know lots of everyday hockey heroes. I come across them all the time in my job as the so-called Hockey Insider. I know how deeply personal their stories are to them and how much those stories have meant to me, too. I am humbled and thankful that when I contacted the following five people to see if they would be interested in sharing their stories, each of them enthusiastically agreed and did such a magnificent job.

- Ben Fanelli's career wasn't in jeopardy as much as his life was—or certainly his quality of life—but his story of returning to the game after severe on-ice head trauma and starting a foundation to help empower others in need is a testament to incredible will, determination and character. He's one of the most impressive young men you'll ever meet.

- Dr. Charles Tator, a neurosurgeon from Toronto, has literally tried to piece back together Canada's severely injured children, notably those shattered by catastrophic spinal cord injuries and head trauma. More important, though, Dr. Tator's story is that of Canada's single greatest advocate for player safety and preventive measures from youth sports, most notably hockey, to the NHL.

- Craig Cunningham's story of suffering an acute cardiac event moments before the opening face-off an American Hockey League game and having his leg amputated has been well documented. But losing the only career he ever dreamed of is what has driven him to give his life new meaning. Alongside Dr. Zain Khalpey, the superstar surgeon who saved his life, Craig has established a foundation to prevent others from going through the same thing.

• Hilary Knight could have settled for leading Team USA on the ice, further padding her impressive statistics and reputation as an elite athlete. Instead, Hilary, along with Team USA captain Meghan Duggan and the other women on the national team, took a hard stand and threatened a strike right before the world championships, in order to get better compensation and benefits. Who knew winning an Olympic gold medal would be the second-biggest victory on Hilary's résumé?

I hope you're inspired by these stories. I know I am, because in some way, shape, or form, these people are heroes, maybe not the kind who will get statues or the fleeting glory of a game-winning goal, but heroes for living their best life regardless of any adversity or obstacles, every day.

It's not by accident that the storytellers in this book represent the interests of a wide cross-section of the population—men, women, black, white, Canadian, American, Métis, Punjabi, LGBTQ, immigrants, blind, deaf, disabled, rich, poor. Historically, the founders and longtime shepherds of hockey have been white men, and while I'm proud of the game they built and the traditions that make it so great, the reality is that for a very long time—too long, to be honest—hockey has been a largely homogenized sport. Thankfully, with initiatives like the NHL's Hockey Is for Everyone—which advocates for a safe and positive environment for anyone who is passionate about the game, regardless of race, colour, religion, national origin, gender, disability, sexual orientation, or socioeconomic status—things are changing. If hockey is to survive and thrive in the modern world, if we're going to continue to grow the game, it's absolutely essential that we all do a much better job of being more inclusive, ensuring that the game is open and welcoming to everyone.

This is a truth that's hit home for me over the last number of years. Let me explain.

Growing up in a working-class family in Scarborough, I wasn't poor, but my family certainly wasn't rich, and playing hockey was expensive. When I was young, my dad worked all day on an airplane manufacturing assembly line, and as soon as he got home, my mom would leave for a night shift in the service department of a car dealership—all that to make ends meet, then pay for me to play hockey. It was rare for me to be in the house with both of them at the same time.

When I was one year old, my mom was diagnosed with rheumatoid arthritis, a disease that caused soreness and swelling in the joints of her fingers and toes. Gradually, her hands, feet, knees, elbows, and every other joint in her body became a gnarled mess of searing pain, even after multiple surgeries. Every second of every day and night was hard, hard as hell.

When her arthritis no longer permitted her to work, my dad got a part-time job at the same car dealership my mom had worked at. Once he finished his day job at the De Havilland Aircraft Company, he would head over to the dealership for a few hours. He'd be gone by seven a.m. each day and wouldn't get home until nine o'clock each night. When he was home, he was caring for my mother, whose rheumatoid arthritis eventually put her in a wheelchair and, at age fifty-four, killed her.

I grew up in a house where my mom was constantly in pain and my dad was always working, and yet neither of them ever complained or felt sorry for themselves. They just did what had to be done and still gave me all the love and support I needed.

I never had to look too far for heroes in my house.

I like to think I inherited a strong work ethic from my parents. As I made my way in journalism, specifically hockey journalism, I was driven. I climbed the ladder, got good jobs, and over time, by any objective measure, I achieved a degree of status and some success within the media and hockey community. While I consider it a great privilege to have attained the position I have today, at no time did I ever feel privileged, at least not in the sense that anything was handed to me. But now that I'm a little older, a little wiser, and a lot less self-absorbed, I know that's not entirely true.

What has come sharply into focus for me over the last decade or so is that while my parents made sacrifices and I did work harder than most and I did earn everything I've got, my success came easier to me than others.

I didn't have to battle the racism that Wayne Simmonds experienced and no doubt still does.

I never had to walk a mile in Kevin Monkman's shoes.

I worked hard and made sacrifices to make my way in my career, but never as hard or as many as Harnarayan Singh.

I had none of the physical challenges or adversity faced by Greg Westlake, Christian Holmes, or Wayne St. Denis.

I never had to worry about whether I was getting shortchanged on my pay or benefits because I was a woman, like Hilary Knight.

I didn't have anyone doubting my place on a hockey broadcast simply because I was a woman, like Andi Petrillo.

I was never made to feel like an outsider in the game I loved, like Brock McGillis.

I like to think that if I had, I would have done the same as they did: dug in, made my way, and used our game's shared values to overcome those obstacles and then, after finally achieving a measure of success, paid it forward and shared that success to make our hockey community a stronger place. Because these stories aren't just about persevering or beating the odds. They're about doing all that but also about giving back and building a sense of community to make our corner of the world a far better place.

That, ultimately, is why I chose to be part of *Everyday Hockey Heroes*.

I knew that if I was going to be involved with this book, I had to have a personal connection with the stories. My good friend Jim Lang, an accomplished broadcaster and author, interviewed almost everyone you'll meet in these pages and helped them all share their stories, and I wanted to contribute in a significant way, too. I wanted to write the introduction, and I wanted to write the final chapter on my pal Kevin Brown, whose story I've wanted to tell for a while.

Kevin is a farmer in rural Ontario, not too far from Stratford. He was an on-ice hockey official, too. Until that fateful day, December 29, 2009, when he almost died on the ice and his life forever changed. On one level, Kevin's story could be viewed as tragic, but I see an inspiring young man who reminds us just how fragile life is. In a mere fraction of a second, it can all change so fast. *Memento mori*.

For Kevin, it wasn't to be that day. So he carries on, as did Jonathan Pitre, as do the survivors of the Broncos' bus crash, as we all do, really. Because life isn't about the fleeting glory of a game-winning goal; it's about living a purposeful life, regardless of adversity or obstacle. It's about trying our best to be everyday hockey heroes.

Bob McKenzie

EVERYDAY HOCKEY HEROES

Wayne's Road
Hockey Warriors

Wayne Simmonds

There's an old saying that it takes a village to raise a child.
Scarborough definitely raised me as a hockey player, and
I'm so proud that I get to be a part of that community.

Some of my earliest memories are of my dad taking me skating at our local outdoor rink in Scarborough, Ontario. Every Saturday morning, without fail, my dad would knock on my bedroom door.

"Wayne, let's get going! We're going skating."

"It's freezing out there, Dad," I'd say, covering myself in a warm blanket. "I don't want to go."

"You'll have fun once you get out there and get moving. And we can get some hot chocolate afterward, okay?"

Yes, hot chocolate, the magic words. Somehow the thought of it would always get me out of bed, into the car, and onto the rink. And my dad was right. Even though it was so cold I could see my breath in front of me, once I'd laced up my skates and done a few laps, I was the happiest kid on the ice. It was there on that little outdoor rink with my dad that my love of hockey began.

But playing the game wasn't always easy. My family is African Nova Scotian, and I often wondered if I fit in the world of hockey, which was, and still is, a very white sport. On Saturday nights, our family would crowd around the TV to watch the hockey game, and I'd wonder if guys who looked like me could play in the NHL. There weren't many, but when I saw what Jarome Iginla or Mike Grier could do on the ice, I started to believe it was possible.

And the tipping point came when I attended a hockey camp in Scarborough run by Kevin Weekes, who at that time was playing for the Tampa Bay Lightning. I always looked up to Kevin. He was a black guy who grew up in Scarborough, just like me. Meeting guys like Kevin and Anson Carter, another black NHLer from Toronto, was incredible—these were professional hockey players and they were talking to me! That day, I started thinking about my future, and I allowed myself to believe that the colour of my skin wasn't a barrier and if I gave the game my all, I could play in the NHL, too.

I had been playing AA hockey for five years when I went to try out for the Wexford Raiders, an AAA team in the elite Greater Toronto Hockey League (GTHL). I remember walking into the dressing room and seeing that all the other kids there had brand-new equipment, including these sweet composite sticks. I knew I was a good player and that I had talent, but I couldn't help but notice that all my gear, from my skates to my wooden stick, was secondhand. I'm from a big family of seven, and my parents, Cyril and Wanda, are some of the hardest-working people I know. My dad was in construction and my mom worked for the city of Toronto and went to school full-time. They did the best they could for us, but by the time the bills were paid, there wasn't a lot of money left over for things like new skates and sticks, so I was used to wearing hand-me-downs.

As much as I wanted a new composite stick like the other guys, playing hockey with my buddies was more important, and I had to focus on the tryout if I wanted to move up with them in the league. I took a deep breath, pushed the image of all that flashy new gear out of my mind, and skated my heart out. And I made it! I made a team, and a really good one at that. My dream of playing for the NHL was that much closer.

As I came out of that rink, one of my friends, and now a fellow Raider, told me that our coach had asked to see me. I walked up to our car, where my mom was waiting, and started putting my equipment into the trunk.

"Hey Mom, I gotta go back up. Coach wants to see me."

"Okay, but before we go in, I need to talk to you about something."

"This sounds serious," I said, hopping in the front seat.

"It is." She looked down at her hands. "Honey, we are so proud of you and your accomplishments, but AAA is a lot of money and your father and I aren't sure we'll be able to afford it this year."

"Oh." It was all I could say.

My mom explained some of the realities of our family's finances, how the cost to register to play AAA was so much higher than AA, how even then my coaches were helping my parents out by lowering rates and my teammates' parents were helping with rides to tournaments. Even with all that support, we didn't have the money for AAA.

"Do you still want to go and talk to the coach?"

"No, I don't think so," I said. She started the car and we drove home in silence.

As disappointed as I was in that moment, I was determined to make it to AAA someday. I worked every job I could to save the money. I even sold chocolates one summer, but it still wasn't enough. Five years went by. When I turned sixteen, I was asked to try out for the Toronto Junior Canadiens, which is one of the best AAA teams in the GTHL. I went to my parents to have a heart-to-heart.

"Mom, Dad, I need to talk about the tryouts next spring."

They exchanged a look. This had been on their minds, too. I plowed on.

"I know we haven't been able to pay for AAA in the past, but is there any way we can make it work this year? I feel like this is my last shot to get noticed by scouts from the juniors. And if I got drafted to a junior team, you wouldn't have to pay for any more fees."

Back then, once you were in Junior A, the league offered sponsorships.

My dad let out a sigh. "We've discussed this before, Wayne. It's a lot of money."

"What if I can pay half the fees? I can work construction with you, Dad, to make the money. I know if I get into AAA, I'll get to the juniors." *And one step closer to the NHL*, I thought.

My mom put a hand on my dad's arm. "Cyril, maybe we can make this work. Maybe we can get sponsors. Every time we've asked for help, people come through. That's what this community is all about."

"All right." My dad smiled. "Let's do it."

"Yes!" I cheered. "Thank you so much! I won't let you down." I turned to leave, but my mom's voice stopped me.

"Wayne, we know you want to play in the NHL. If you do make it, there are two things I want you to do."

"Okay."

"I want you to give back to your community, and I want you to give to your church."

"Yes, Mom. Of course. *When* I make it to the NHL, I'll give back." The NHL was still a ways off, but it meant so much that my parents believed in me.

I was busy, to say the least. I was waking up at five a.m. to go to work with my dad. In between high school classes and hockey practice, I was squeezing in extra construction shifts whenever I could. I saved every dollar, and when I tried out for the Junior Canadiens that

*Here I am with the Toronto Aces celebrating
our city championship win against the
Vaughan Panthers. This was the year
before I moved up to the AAA level.*

spring, I not only made the team, but I had my half of the money—
$3,000—to pay the fees. The manual labour had the added bonus
of getting me in great shape, and I had a strong season—nobody
pushed me off the puck that year!

Our hard work paid off, too. At our all-Ontario playoffs, Mike
McCourt, the head coach for the Brockville Braves, saw me play and
asked me to come to Brockville for a tryout. After I did, he offered
me a spot on his team. I was in the juniors! My parents were thrilled
that we'd made it this far together.

It all felt a little surreal. I remember walking into the dressing
room for the first time and seeing my sweater hanging on my stall.
We had new equipment, too—all the composite sticks a guy could
want!

From there, things started happening for me. In 2006, I was drafted by the Owen Sound Attack, a really good team in the Ontario Hockey League (OHL). Even when I was playing in the OHL, I couldn't forget about Scarborough, though. My buddies were part of a summer league ball hockey team, and it looked like so much fun that I joined them. In the off-seasons, I'd stay fit by chasing a ball inside a local rink on a hot and humid day—the opposite of those freezing-cold mornings with my dad when I was a kid.

It was on one such summer Saturday in 2007 that I received a phone call that changed my life. It was from Mike Futa, the former GM of the Owen Sound Attack and the current head of amateur scouting for the LA Kings.

"They want you, Wayne. You can score goals and skate fast. And you're tough enough to stand up for your teammates."

"This is a dream come true, Mike! Thank you."

It took a moment to sink in that I had made the LA Kings as a twenty-year-old rookie and that I was being paid to play hockey.

As soon as I heard the news that I had been drafted, I called my parents.

"I have big news! I got into the NHL! The LA Kings want me."

All I could hear was a big sob on the other line. "Oh, Wayne," my mom started. "I'm so proud of you."

There was a cough, then my dad spoke. "Way to go. I knew you could do it." His voice was eerily calm.

Was he trying not to cry? I wondered. "Just think, a few years earlier we couldn't afford AAA. Now I'm in the NHL," I said. "I couldn't have done this without all your support, guys. You sacrificed so much for me."

"You worked hard, Wayne. You earned this," my mom said.

I couldn't stop smiling. Anything was truly possible.

I had so much to thank my parents for, but if it wasn't for the help from those in our hockey community in Scarborough, I would never have made it to the NHL. They gave me the chance to play the game I love. I knew I had to honour my promise to my mom to give back, but at first, I didn't know what I could do.

After my fourth year in the NHL, I was traded from the LA Kings to the Philadelphia Flyers. By then, I was an established professional athlete making a good living. I got in touch with Brandon Sinclair, a friend of mine from my minor-league hockey days in Scarborough. Both of our families struggled to put us through hockey, and it was the support of the community that allowed us to continue to play. The costs have only risen since then.

We got to talking about how great the hockey camps we went to as kids were, how seeing the NHLers motivated us, and we decided that we should do something similar to grow the game and support the next generation of Canadian hockey players. We wanted to make a difference in the lives of underprivileged kids and give them the opportunity to learn and play hockey.

I was also inspired by Willie O'Ree, the first black player in the NHL and the head of the league's diversity program, so one of my personal goals for a hockey camp was to get other NHL players who look like me involved in the camp and show the kids from visible minorities that hockey is an option for them, that hockey is for everyone. Inclusivity will only make the sport itself better.

Together Brandon and I started Wayne's Road Hockey Warriors, a charity ball hockey tournament for Scarborough kids to meet and play with NHL stars. The summer of 2012, we launched our first event. I'll never forget that day.

I walked into the Scarborough Gardens Arena—where years earlier I had played—nervous about how the day was going to go, but excited to meet the kids and the parents who were huddled in little groups around the arena. I went over to one.

Posing with the winning team at the fifth annual tournament.

"Hey, guys, I'm Wayne. How are you all doing today?" I held out my hand to fist-bump one of the boys who looked to be about eight or nine. He shyly nudged my hand back.

The rest of the group exchanged furtive looks and whispers until one of the moms behind the kids stepped forward.

"Sorry, I think they're a little starstruck."

"Oh." I was shocked. To me, it didn't feel that long ago that I was their age and at a hockey camp.

"It's okay. I'm sure they'll loosen up," she continued. "Wayne, we're all just so thrilled about what you're doing here. Thank you!"

"It's my pleasure. This community has always taken care of me, so it's important to me to give back." I looked down at the kids. "Okay, are you guys ready to play some hockey?"

"Yeah!" they cheered.

After we introduced the kids to Drew Doughty and Chris and Anthony Stewart, we gave them new gloves, helmets, sticks, jerseys, and a good bag. Then we divided them up into groups to play hockey. In no time, the arena was filled with the sound of sticks slapping the floor, and man, did we have fun. It was so rewarding to see the smiles on their faces when they mastered a stickhandling move or scored a goal. The best moment was awarding the Wayne's Road Hockey Warriors' trophy to the winning team.

Throughout the day we hosted raffles for equipment and other prizes, signed autographs, and took lots of pictures. Everything went off without a hitch, and we've never looked back since. We've now hosted six tournaments and raised approximately $100,000. We've been able to sponsor over forty kids so they can play hockey without worrying about equipment or registration fees. And with all the donations from the NHL Players' Association, Bauer, and Warrior Sports, we've given over 550 kids free equipment.

I've invited Tyler Seguin, Darnell Nurse, Jordan Subban, Joel

This candid photo was taken during the celebrity game finale at the second annual Wayne's Road Hockey Warriors tournament. I had just scored a goal and was celebrating my victory.

Ward, Devante Smith-Pelly, and many other guys from all over the NHL to come to our tournament, and they always say yes. They want to give back, too. As do the kids. A lot of them come back to work as counsellors. The cycle of hockey is like the cycle of life. As you gain more experience, you try to pass that knowledge on to others.

Whenever parents tell me how much they appreciate the camp, I think of how these parents belong to the same community that stepped in to help me when I was growing up, donating used equipment, taking me to games and practices. Hockey is so much about the togetherness of a community. It was through them and through hockey that I learned I could do anything if I put my heart and soul into it. And that's the real goal of the camp: to show the kids that they can do whatever they put their mind to.

I was able to keep my promise to my mom and give back to the community that helped me achieve my dream. Now my new dream is to see someone from the camp make it to the NHL. Someday I hope one of the kids skates by me during an NHL game and says, "Do you remember me? I went to one of your camps." And then gives me a big cross-check in the back.

There's an old saying that it takes a village to raise a child. Scarborough definitely raised me as a hockey player, and I'm so proud that I get to be a part of that community.

Wayne Simmonds is an alternate captain for the Philadelphia Flyers. He's affectionately known by his teammates and fans as "Wayne Train." He played for Team Canada at the 2008 Ice Hockey World Junior Championships, where they won gold. In 2012, he started Wayne's Road Hockey Warriors. To find out more about Wayne and his charity, follow him on Twitter at @Simmonds17.

All Heart

Craig Cunningham

Since I was a kid, I've loved hockey for the game itself—for
that indescribable feeling when you put the puck in the net.
Now, though, I also love hockey for the family it's given me.

My mom thought I was dead when they brought me off the ice. Later, the doctors said that my heart had stopped for eighty-three minutes. To this day, no one knows why I suddenly went into cardiac arrest on November 19, 2016. I was twenty-six, in perfect health, and had just been named captain of the Tucson Roadrunners.

I remember waking up in a hospital bed and grabbing the first person I saw. "Who are you?" I asked, taking in the white coat I clutched in my hands.

"My name is Dr. Zain Khalpey," the man replied, unfazed by my sudden interrogation. He seemed happy to see me moving. "And you're at Banner University Medical Center in Tucson, Arizona."

That's when I noticed my mom, Heather, standing next to the doctor. She was in tears. "You survived the surgery. You're alive!"

I wanted to console her, to tell her I was all right, but I had no idea what was going on. "What surgery?"

"You've just undergone emergency heart surgery, Craig," Dr. Khalpey answered. "You suffered a cardiac arrest on the ice."

"On the ice?"

"You were lining up for the face-off when all of a sudden you were on your back." My mom took my hand in hers. "I was so scared."

"You were lucky, Craig. The firefighters from the pregame ceremony had been standing just a few feet away from you when you collapsed," Dr. Khalpey said. "They were able to start CPR immediately." He went on to explain that the emergency responders performed CPR the entire way to the hospital. "When I saw you, they'd been working on you for almost an hour and a half. That's unheard of."

I had so many questions, but as Dr. Khalpey spoke, a sense of calm came over me and I knew I was in good hands. In the days and weeks that followed, I would come to realize that without all the first responders at the arena, I would have died on the ice, and without Dr. Khalpey, I would have died on the operating table.

My mom got me on skates when I was just two years old, and since then hockey has always been a part of my life. I grew up in the small town of Trail, British Columbia, where in the winter, you either skied or played hockey—that was all there was to do. My dad, Alvin, was a skier, but my older brother, Ryan, my younger brother, Mitchel, and I preferred hockey.

"I'm going to be a hockey player," I said to anyone who listened. "I'm going to play in the NHL."

It never occurred to me that anything could jeopardize that dream. But then the unthinkable happened. My dad died in a car accident. I was just five years old, too young to remember my dad well, but my mom says I used to follow him around everywhere, and that without him, I was a little lost.

I imagine my mother felt my father's loss ten times more. When Mitchel had been born, my parents had made the decision that my father would provide for the family and my mother would raise us

*Here I am posing on my best friend Paul Mailey's
outdoor rink his dad used to make every winter.*

boys and take care of the home. Now that my father was gone, she
was a single parent of three young boys without an income.

She opened a day care in our house so that she could be at home
with Ryan, Mitchel, and me. She'd see us off to school in the morning, then look after eight to ten other kids all day until we came
home. She never got a break, but I never heard her complain or saw
her struggle. She is the epitome of resilience. We still didn't have a lot
of money, but somehow my mom always found a way to make ends
meet and keep us boys in hockey.

"I'm going to pay you back one day, Mom," I said to her whenever
she paid my hockey fees or drove me to a practice or game.

"Don't think about that, Craig. I want you to have fun," she always
replied.

A few years after my dad passed away, Ray Ferraro, a Trail native
and former NHLer, took me under his wing. He treated me like one
of his own sons and helped buy my hockey equipment so I could

keep playing. Whenever he spoke, I listened. He would later go on to become one of my coaches and mentors.

Hockey was an outlet for me—making it to the NHL was all I thought about, and I poured myself into the game. I wasn't naturally gifted, so improving my skills was a grind, but there was nothing I loved more. Every morning before school, I woke up early and shot one hundred to two hundred pucks in the garage. When I came home from school, I'd shoot a few hundred more. Every Wednesday and Sunday, I went to the public skate at the local arena to practice my edgework so I could increase my speed. If no one else showed up, I would bring out my stick and puck and work on my stickhandling. I'd often try to drag Ryan or Mitchel with me so I could practice eluding a defenceman. I like to think I got my sense of discipline and dedication from my mother.

By the time I was thirteen years old, all my hard work—and my mother's sacrifices—started to pay off, and I was making a name for myself in Trail, to the point that I was invited to play a tournament in Vancouver with some of the top Bantam players in the province. I was thrilled at the opportunity, but I had doubts about my ability to compete against the kids from bigger cities.

"Do you think I'll be able to hold my own in Vancouver?" I asked my mom one day. "I'm sure there's more competition."

"You work harder on your skills than anyone else, Craig," she said. "Trust yourself and you'll do just fine."

She was right, as always. I played well and kept up with the big-city kids. That experience really opened my eyes to my future in hockey. *I don't know about the NHL*, I thought. *But I'm definitely going to make it to the juniors.*

I kept practicing my shots in the garage and skating twice a week, and when the 2005 draft rolled around, I sat at one of the computers in my school refreshing the website until there it was: my name.

I had been selected by the Vancouver Giants of the Western Hockey League. I immediately phoned my mom to tell her the good news.

"Mom, the Giants drafted me!" I could barely hold in my excitement.

"Craig, I'm so proud of you," she said. I could sense her smiling over the phone, and I knew she was relieved, too. Even if I didn't go pro, I would have college paid for through the WHL's scholarship program, and after everything my mom had sacrificed for me, it was the least I could do. Without her, I wouldn't have had the opportunity.

I was just sixteen when I moved to Vancouver to play with the Giants, and I still had a lot to learn about hockey and about life. My rookie year was tough—I didn't score a single goal, and scoring had always been something that I had prided myself on. It was the reason I spent all those hours in my garage shooting pucks. I felt like I was letting my team down, and even worse, I felt like I was letting my family down. They had sacrificed so much for me to get there, and I didn't want to waste the opportunity they'd given me. *This can't be the end of the road for me,* I thought.

My teammate Milan Lucic would always remind me that I had potential. "I've seen you score, Craig. You have a great shot."

Milan was an excellent leader, and his vote of confidence went a long way toward rebuilding my self-esteem and making me feel like I was a part of the team.

"You may not be as big as the other guys on the ice," my coach, Don Hay, told me, "but you play hard and gritty. You keep doing what you're doing and you'll get there."

I had a great support system, and I never felt like I was on my own. That summer, Ray opened his Vancouver home to me so that I could live and train with his son, Landon. I doubled down on my effort and spent endless hours on the ice working on my skills. I was learning to be patient on and off the ice, and by the next year, I was racking up points.

In 2008, I was eligible for the NHL draft. This was the moment I had dreamed about since my mom taught me to skate all those years ago. I knew I wasn't going to be a first-round pick, but I was hopeful that someone would give me a chance.

But I was passed over, and the rejection stung. I went back to the Giants, where I was getting more and more ice time and working hard in the off-season to keep myself in peak condition. The next year, when the draft rolled around, I figured I had better odds of being chosen. But again, no team wanted to take a chance on me. I had two more years left with the Giants, and I wanted to make sure they were my best.

I was invited to the New York Rangers' development camp on a tryout basis, and I got an eye-opening look at what it takes to

During my first year with the Vancouver Giants, the team won the Memorial Cup. We're celebrating being the major junior ice hockey champions of the Canadian Hockey League in this photo. I'm second from the left.

become an NHL player. I'd always thought I worked hard, but at the Rangers camp, I learned I would have to dig even deeper if I was going to make it to the NHL. I gave everything I had during that next season with the Giants, and I finished with 37 goals and 60 assists, ranking first in team scoring and sixth in the league—a long way from that goalless rookie year.

Still, as the 2010 NHL draft approached, I didn't think I stood much of a chance. I was nineteen and had only one more year with the Giants to show what I was capable of on the ice before I was too old to be eligible for the draft. If I hadn't wowed the big teams yet, I probably wouldn't this year, I thought.

"I don't think a pick is in the cards for me," I told my mom. "I think I can get into another camp, though. Maybe next year after I'm a free agent, someone will give me an opportunity, and I'll work my way up from there."

"Don't worry about it, Craig," she said. "All that matters is that you're having fun."

I knew I wasn't going to be a first-round pick, so I flew home from Vancouver on the Friday of the draft to surprise my mom. The next day, we watched the following rounds together on the computer. I didn't want many people there in case I didn't get picked at all.

The second and third rounds went by and my name wasn't called. Then I heard my phone ping. It was a message from the GM of the Vancouver Giants.

"Congrats, Craig!" it read.

What is he congratulating me for? I looked up at the computer and saw my name pop up on the screen. I had been drafted by the Boston Bruins.

"Oh my god!" I yelled, still not quite believing what I was seeing.

"I'm so proud of you!" my mom said, giving me a hug. "Your dad would be, too."

I nodded, swallowing hard. She had given up so much for me to pursue my dream. "I won't let you down."

I signed my contract with the Bruins on July 14, 2011, and shortly after I was off to Boston to take part in the team's rookie camp. Development camps are hard, and the Bruins' camp was no exception. We had early-morning practices, extra practices, and even a couple of days of military training. After the camp, I went back to Vancouver and started training harder than ever so I could compete with the best players in the world. That September, I returned for training camp and was on the same ice as the players I had grown up watching: Patrice Bergeron, Tuukka Rask. I was nearly speechless when Cam Neely stopped by the dressing room to talk to us. And I knew Zdeno Chara was big, but in person, he's huge—it seemed like he could stand on the far blue line and reach across to the other blue line with his stick. He covered the entire neutral zone. After a couple of days skating with these all-stars, it hit me that I was competing against these players for a full-time job in the NHL.

Sadly, I didn't make the cut. After the camp, the Bruins sent me back to the juniors. I returned for another development camp the next summer, and after that, I signed a contract to play on their farm team, the Providence Bruins. I still had work to do before I could play with the big club, but I knew I had made a significant step forward. Whenever I doubted if I could make it, I would remember my mom grinding her way through hardships to build a happy life for us. *If I keep at it, I'll succeed, and then I can give her something in return.*

After three years on the farm team, where I matured as a person and a player, I was finally called up to the Bruins, and in my second season with them, I scored my first NHL goal. We were playing the Ottawa Senators, and their centerman Kyle Turris, a fellow BC boy, bobbled the puck at our blue line.

I grabbed the puck, took off at full speed toward the net, and wound up my stick for a slap shot—probably my first in four years. The puck went in! The first thought I had was of my mom and my brothers watching the TV at home. I knew they'd be cheering me on. Then, Kevin Miller, whom I'd lived with our first two years of pro hockey, was hugging me.

"Yeah, man!" he shouted, knocking my helmet with his glove. "You did it!"

That was a special moment. I was evolving into a depth forward with a lot of energy, and I finally had a NHL goal to show for it.

In early 2015, the Boston Bruins put me on waivers, which meant my contract was up for grabs for other NHL teams. I can't say that I was thrilled or surprised—the Bruins were a strong, established team, but a tough one to break into, and I had to fight to stay in the lineup. When the Arizona Coyotes claimed me, I was excited, because their club was still building itself, which meant I would have a better chance at getting time on the ice. They were extremely supportive of my career, and even though I spent the next two years bouncing back and forth between the Coyotes and their minor-league team, I was happy to be in the professional hockey world. The more I played, the more I felt I had a strong chance of staying there. I was at the top of my game, and other than a few bumps and bruises, I was in the best shape of my life. Until I went into cardiac arrest.

I don't remember falling to the ice or even getting ready in the locker room before the game. My last memory is of playing hockey the weekend before. And then I woke up in the hospital with no idea what had happened in the last four days.

My mom told me just how close I had come to dying. At 7:45 p.m., Dr. Khalpey got a call from Dr. George Haloftis, a physician at St. Mary's Hospital. The first responders had gotten me there, but I wasn't responding to medication.

"He'll need more extreme measures if he's to live," Dr. Haloftis said to Dr. Khalpey. "Can you come?"

Dr. Khalpey didn't hesitate. "I'll be right there."

He jumped in his car and raced to St. Mary's, but not before stopping at his own hospital to pick up an extracorporeal membrane oxygenation (ECMO) machine. He was still on his way when he got another call.

"We've had first responders performing chest compressions for an hour already," Dr. Haloftis reported. "He's bleeding from his lungs."

"Don't give up him. I'm almost there."

Dr. Khalpey ran through the hospital doors only to be greeted by forty hockey players and my mom. She told me she had never seen someone so confident and calm.

"Are you Heather? Are you Craig's mom?" he asked.

"I am," she said.

"I'm Zain Khalpey. I'm really good at what I do, and I'm going to save your son."

My mom says she instantly trusted him.

"Craig's organs are failing. We need to get him onto a machine that will act as his heart and lungs and keep his blood pumping. It's called an ECMO," he explained. "It's a risky procedure, but there's no other option."

"Do it. Do whatever you have to."

With my mom's blessing, Dr. Khalpey rushed me into the operating room and successfully stabilized my organs. Once I had been stabilized, I was moved to Banner University Medical Center, where Dr. Khalpey worked so that he could monitor my progress. But a day and a half later, my condition had worsened—my heart was still enlarged and the circulation to my legs had been cut off.

"Heather, I have one more thing I can try."

"What is it?"

"I can make a hole in Craig's heart and decompress the organ," he said. "It's only been done three times before, all by me, but all successful surgeries."

It was a lot of information for my mom to take in.

"I have to do this. Do you trust me?"

"I do."

When Dr. Khalpey brought me into surgery, my heart was black and blue with almost zero function. A few hours after he stitched me back up, my heart was beating on its own.

After I heard the lengths he had gone to save my life, I said, "You're like the Sidney Crosby of cardiac surgeons, Dr. Khalpey."

"I just did my job, Craig. I'm happy you're alive."

"Do you know why this happened to me?" I asked. It was the one question that still troubled me.

"We don't. All your testing came back clear. There are no irregularities with your heart."

That was good news, of course, but it unnerved me that something so catastrophic had been out of my control. I didn't have too much time to dwell on that thought, though, because my battle wasn't over yet. When my heart stopped, my legs hadn't been getting enough blood, and as a result, I'd developed a serious infection in my left leg. The doctors were doing everything they could to clear the infection, but nothing was working. They needed to amputate.

"It's life or limb," they said.

The news hit me hard. Losing a part of my leg would mean losing my hockey career. How could the game I loved be taken away from me so quickly? Suddenly I had to reevaluate my future. For so long, hockey had been my sole focus, but I wanted to live the rest of my life, even if that meant never lacing up my skates again.

Thankfully, my mom was beside me. We talked about my early

days playing hockey, remembered the highlights—my first NHL goal—and thought about my future. There were a lot of tears. I know it hurt her to see my dream cut short, but she really is the strongest person I know, and I think she knew that I would be as relentless about my recovery as I had been about hockey. I felt like my whole life was about to change.

Christmas Eve, the day of the surgery, was by far the hardest. I could see the pain in my mom's eyes, and I wanted to comfort her.

"I'm going to be fine. I'll get better," I said. "It could be worse." Brave words, but deep down, I was so damn scared. I had no idea what was coming my way.

No one wanted to risk my heart, so the orthopedic surgeon used local anesthesia instead. Fortunately, Dr. Khalpey was by my side during the whole procedure, which eased some of my nerves.

The days that followed were the toughest I've ever had. Giving up hockey was one thing, but as I lay there in my hospital bed, all I could think was if I would ever be able to walk again.

Shortly after my surgery, a fellow amputee—and triathlete—came to visit me.

"I understand what you're going through, Craig," he said. "But you have to know that losing your leg is not the end of your active lifestyle. You can still do everything that you used to."

Ray also came to see me. "I know hockey is your identity, but even the guys with long careers have to face the day when they're over," he said. "No one can ever take your career away from you, Craig. You made it to the NHL. You did what you set out to do. And you're strong enough to discover a life outside the game, too."

I'd always looked up to Ray as a mentor, so his encouragement meant the world to me. I began to realize that I was incredibly lucky to have lived the life I did and that there was so much more out there for me beyond hockey.

People from all corners of the league—including those I had never met or even played with—reached out to let me know that they were thinking of me and were there for anything I might need. Even though I'd played only two years with the Arizona Coyotes organization, the entire staff showered me with unwavering support. They arranged hotel rooms in Tucson for my family and friends who were visiting me in the hospital, and they helped me in countless other ways. I realized that getting claimed off waivers by the Coyotes was one of the best things that could have happened to me. The overwhelming response from everyone in the hockey community inspired me to pick myself up and move forward.

My mom was a constant support. I continued to have issues with my leg and underwent several more surgeries, which slowed my recovery. Whenever I was too tired to do my rehab, she held me

My mom has never left my side. In March 2017, just four months after my accident, I returned to the Tucson arena with her to thank the team and the community for their continued support.

accountable. If I was having a bad day, I had a few choice words for her, but that never fazed her.

"You can't let losing your leg define you," she told me.

I knew that in her own way she was telling me to get to work, and I took her advice and buckled down, spending endless hours learning how to walk with a prosthetic leg. In some ways, it was like shooting pucks in the garage as a kid—I'd spend hour after hour focused on one simple motion, pushing my body and mind to perfect it. It felt good to be striving for a goal once more.

After twelve weeks, I walked for the first time. The pain was unlike anything I had experienced before. Just taking a few steps was excruciating. *I hope it won't always be like this*, I thought. I kept with my rehab and started walking farther and farther as the pain receded. A month later, I got back into my skates.

I was nervous about skating again, but after watching hundreds of videos of men and women with prosthetic limbs tackle what seemed like impossible feats, I knew I had to try. Stepping onto the rink and hearing the sound of my skates on the ice beneath me was the best healing I could have asked for. Skating had always been my passion, and knowing I could still have it helped me overcome a mental barrier.

Life isn't so different now. If anything, it has taken on new meaning.

For one, Dr. Khalpey and I have remained close since that first meeting, when I greeted him with a chokehold.

"I'm disappointed that we weren't able to save your leg," he said to me once. "You're a hockey player."

"Without you and your team, I wouldn't even be here," I replied. "You gave me a second chance. And you made one of the most difficult experiences of my life bearable."

He smiled. "Just doing my job."

I spent my whole life surrounded by athletes but never knew the risk of sudden cardiac arrest until I was affected by it. When I was, I was lucky to have a whole team of first responders at hand and the best doctor in the world waiting in the wings. Not everyone gets that, though. So, Dr. Khalpey and I created the All Heart Foundation, a nonprofit aimed at preventing sudden cardiac arrests by promoting regular screenings to diagnose those at risk. We are currently working with engineers to use the heart monitor app on smartwatches as an early detection system for abnormalities, and we're also in the process of implementing a fingerprick test before and after workouts to check blood levels for irregularities. People often think heart attacks happen only to someone who is elderly or unhealthy, but that's not always the case. No one is invincible, and my goal is to improve the precision and frequency of heart screenings for future hockey players. If we can prevent one person from having a sudden cardiac arrest, then it will be worth it.

Since I was a kid, I've loved hockey for that indescribable feeling when you put the puck in the net—for the game. Now, though, I also love hockey for the family it's given me. The same sport that spurs professional competition also fosters a sense of community unlike anything I've ever experienced before.

I now work as a scout for the Coyotes, which makes me feel like I'm still a part of the game. I like to think I have an advantage because I competed with some of the players I'm evaluating, and sharing the ice is the best way to gauge a player's ability. When I see a player who's lacking in one skill but makes up for it with the rest of his game, I remember my own struggles as a junior with the Giants. I miss those days, and I miss playing, but I'm thankful to have a new opportunity in the game that brings me to the rink, and whenever I can, I lace up my skates and get back on the ice. At the

When I was well enough to leave the hospital, I made sure to visit the Tucson firefighters who had helped keep me alive.

end of the day, though, it's a game, and the life outside it is just as important.

Tucson is a special place to me. In my moment of need, the entire town came to my rescue. I've been to the fire hall to visit the team that saved my life and to learn CPR from the best first responders I know.

I still have regular checkups with Dr. Khalpey. We talk almost every day, and my mom and I spent Thanksgiving with him and his family. He's even invited me to watch one of his surgeries. I'm excited to see his magic hands in action, but I know I will be looking at the person he's operating on and thinking that it wasn't that long ago that I was on the table with my life hanging in the balance. There's no trophy in the NHL that would be good enough to pay tribute to Dr. Khalpey for everything he's done for me.

I still have bad days when my leg is sore because I've overdone a workout or haven't taken the time to rest. But most days, I wake up with a smile on my face, feeling lucky to be alive and surrounded by the people I love.

Craig Cunningham is a former NHL centreman who played for the Boston Bruins and the Arizona Coyotes. In 2017, he was awarded the prestigious Fred T. Hunt Memorial Award, given to the American Hockey League player who best exemplifies the qualities of sportsmanship, determination, and dedication to hockey. He currently serves as a pro scout for the Coyotes. He lives in Tucson, Arizona. Learn more about the All Heart Foundation at www.allheartfoundation.org, and follow Craig on Instagram @craig.cunningham14.

The Hockey Sledgehammer

Greg Westlake

If I'm going to play sledge hockey, I'm going to be the best sledge hockey player out there. I'm not dabbling with the sport on weekends. I'm going to make it to Team Canada.

I can't remember a time when I didn't love hockey. I'm the youngest of four kids, and even as a toddler, I followed my siblings around and tried to do everything they were doing. My older brother, Scott, played the game, and I, being a typical youngest sibling, wanted nothing more than to follow in his footsteps. By the time I was three, I was skating at the local rink in rural Ottawa. I was hooked the second I got on the ice. There's nothing quite like the rush of air on your face as you race down the ice or the satisfaction of hitting the top corner with a wrist shot, although I usually played in net because I wasn't fast enough to compete the way I wanted to. Still, when I was playing hockey, I felt like I was the same as every other kid, even though I knew I was different.

When I was born, I was missing a tibia in one leg and a fibula in the other, and as a result, my feet were malformed. The doctors told my parents, Jim and Deb, that my feet would never be fully functional and that the best way forward was to perform a double amputation below each knee so that I could walk with the use of prosthetics when I was older. My parents were devastated. This was

29

not the life they wanted for me, but they knew that surgery was the right decision, so when I was eighteen months old, my lower legs were amputated.

My physical condition could have ruled my life, but I'm stubborn, and there was no way I was going to let my body stop me from doing anything I wanted.

I have my parents to thank for fostering my sense of determination. My parents have an old VHS tape that shows me about two years old bundled up in my winter gear and playing in the snow with my brother and sisters. Like any toddler, I fell down a lot, but because I wore prosthetics, I had a more difficult time learning to walk, let alone standing back up after I fell. When I watch the tape now, one of the first things I notice is how my parents never rushed to help me. I can hear their voices off camera, though.

"You can do it, Greg," my mom says.

And as I get one leg straight under me, my dad chimes in. "That's right. You got it."

I know that holding back their support wasn't easy, but my parents wanted to make sure I learned how to stand on my own, literally. I had to struggle. I had to build my muscles. It was hard, but if I hadn't learned how to pick myself up when I fell down, I wouldn't be where I am today.

I started playing organized hockey when I was five years old. I was the only kid on the ice wearing prosthetics, which were usually decorated with Hockey Canada stickers, but no one could tell, because I wore skates and hockey socks just like everyone else. And skating with prosthetics never felt like work—all I wanted was to have fun with my friends.

Even when I wasn't on the ice, I was a full-blown hockey nerd.

"Who does Wendel Clark play for, Greg?" Scott would quiz me.

"Easy. The Toronto Maple Leafs."

Here I am at four years old.
Whenever there was a chance to
get on the rink, I was there.

"Okay, when was he drafted?"

"Nineteen eighty-five. He was the first-round draft pick." I grinned. "Everyone knows that."

"How many penalties per minute did he have last season?"

"A hundred and fifteen. Do you want to know his height and weight?"

"You know that, too?"

"He's five eleven and weighs 197 pounds."

"Greg, you need to get out more."

"Ask me another question! Choose any guy in the NHL. I'll tell you his stats." And on it would go.

Hockey was a staple of my childhood. My dad worked in insurance, and whenever there was a good opportunity, we would move.

We lived in North Vancouver and Ottawa before finally settling down in Oakville just outside Toronto when I was nine. Everywhere we went, sports were my way of meeting new people and making friends. In Oakville, I played on two roller hockey teams in the summer and I played ice hockey at the local rink all winter, eventually moving out of my usual goalie position to play forward. I don't remember any of my school friends or teammates ever making fun of me. They loved that I was keeping up with them and I loved playing the game. The best was when one of my friends would tell me, "When I'm with you, Greg, I never think of your disability."

At that time, my skills were on par with the other players, and I made it to A level hockey, but I knew I was never going to be able to

During the summers, I kept my skills sharp by playing on roller hockey teams.

play AAA hockey or make it to the juniors. I just couldn't compete at that level.

That was hard for me to accept. I was fifteen and all my friends played hockey. My life revolved around the game. I never felt more Canadian than when I was wearing a jersey and shooting the puck, but I wanted to be a high-performance athlete, the best in a sport.

My parents were my biggest advocates, especially my mom.

"If playing a sport at a high level is really important to you, Greg," she said, "then we can make that happen."

"How?" I asked. "We've tried every sport." And we had, baseball, volleyball, even martial arts.

"We just have to find the right one," she assured me.

A month later, my mom suggested sledge hockey. "This is a good opportunity for you," she said.

"You'll get the chance to really compete," my dad added.

I wasn't so sure. "I've never thought about playing a Paralympic sport. I've always been able to do well in able-bodied sports."

"You can do anything you put your mind to, Greg," my mom said. "I think this will be a good challenge for you and give you what you want. And you can join a recreational team right here in Toronto."

I thought about it for a moment. "Okay, but if I'm going to play sledge hockey, I'm going to be the best sledge hockey player out there. I'm not dabbling with the sport on weekends. I'm going to make it to Team Canada."

Part of me thought that sledge hockey would be easy. I had a solid background in hockey, so I assumed I would step right in and dominate. We got in touch with Cruisers Sports for the Physically Disabled and I went to the Iceland Mississauga arena for a practice. If I liked it, I would join a team within the Ontario Sledge Hockey Association (OSHA).

As soon as I got into the sledge on the ice, I realized how wrong

I'd been about the sport being easy. *Why am I going so slow?* I thought. After twenty minutes, my back and arms were killing me.

While sledge hockey is fundamentally the same as hockey—three periods, five players and a goalie per side, most goals wins—the details are wildly different. The players use different muscle groups and need a unique skill set because they play sitting down in the sledge and propel themselves with sharp picks on the bottom of two sticks. I realized that if I was going to make it to the top of the sport, I'd have to adapt my hockey skills.

That first practice, I remember trying to go for the slot, but by the time I pushed my sledge there, the play was already going the other way. Shooting the puck in stand-up hockey was so simple—just a flick of the wrist. In sledge hockey, it's one of the hardest things to do. First, I had to get close to the net on my sledge using the picks at the bottom of my sticks, then in one motion, I had to turn the stick over to use the blade to shoot the puck. Trust me, it's ten times more difficult to do than it sounds. That first day I managed to get close to the slot and I tried to go top shelf with a shot, but I couldn't raise the puck with one arm. I knew what I wanted to do, but I couldn't execute the play. Playing sledge hockey was a frustrating and humbling experience, especially for someone as competitive as me. But I wasn't about to give up. If anything, I was even more determined.

I started playing with the Mississauga Cruisers, and I quickly began to learn the finer points of sledge hockey. My parents had been right—I needed the challenge and the competition—but I knew I also had to get much stronger if I was to make it to the Paralympics. Upper-body strength is crucial to excelling in sledge hockey, because players use their upper body to skate, stop, and turn, and shoot. When I wasn't at the gym working out, I was at the rink practicing shooting and passing on my sledge. Slowly but surely, my play started to improve, and I was able to keep up with the game.

There was one skill from stand-up hockey that I was able to adapt to sledge hockey easily: checking. Sledge hockey is full contact. The only difference is that in sledge hockey, the players don't just get bruises, we get cuts and scrapes from the sharp picks on the ends of the opposing team's sticks. When we're in a tough game and there's a lot of congestion in the corners or along the boards, players will "pick" each other.

I often tease my mom about how dangerous the sport is.

"When you suggested I play sledge hockey, did you realize there would be picks flying around?" I ask.

"No." She rolls her eyes. "But I'm not worried about you, Greg. You're the toughest player out there."

"So you have absolutely no concerns when I'm on the ice?

"Oh, I do. I worry about the other players you pick!"

We do wear padding, so "picking" isn't as barbaric as it sounds. And I get my fair share of injuries, too. I once ended up with twelve stitches on my forearm from another guy's pick. I looked like someone who lost a sword fight in *Game of Thrones*, but my girlfriend loved it.

A few years after I started playing sledge hockey, the national team got in touch and asked me to come try out. They had just come back from the 2002 Paralympics, where unfortunately they hadn't placed, and they were interested in grooming some younger players. *This is my chance*, I thought.

My mom came with me to the tryout. The team was made up of a lot of talented guys, but I noticed that they weren't that physical on the ice. In my mind, I thought the team could use a little more fire and emotion, so I tried to showcase that when I played.

After the last practice season of the day, the head coach, Jeff Snyder, called me and my mom into the dressing room.

"We really like how you played today, Greg, and we think you have a lot to offer," he said. "Congratulations, you made the team!"

I was over the moon. For so many years, I'd done everything I could to become a top athlete in a sport, but my body had let me down. Finally, I had made it. "Thank you," I said. "Thank you so much."

I looked at my mom, who had tears in her eyes. She understood better than anyone what I had gone through to get to that moment. "I'm so happy for you, Greg. All your hard work is paying off."

"Don't let up on that yet," Jeff cut in. "We need you to be in top form for the 2006 Winter Paralympics in Turin."

That threw me for another loop. I would be representing Canada on the international stage, wearing the same jersey that NHLers like Steve Yzerman and Mario Lemieux had worn. It was a dream come true.

There were a few other rookies on the team, too, but I wanted to make sure I earned my spot, and since I had a natural passion for the role of agitator, I made it my job to ruffle some feathers. Whenever we were playing a game, I'd find the best player on the opposing team and do everything I could to get under his skin. When the ref wasn't looking, I'd get in what checks I could or I'd draw penalties, then try to score on the power play just to drive the other team crazy. I channeled my inner Brad Marchand. I was still a teenager, so being a loudmouth and a troublemaker on the ice came easily, and it bought me time to further develop my stickhandling and scoring skills.

The team was feeling good going into the Paralympics, but missing the podium in 2002 weighed heavily on our minds. Our track record—bronze in 1994 and silver in 1998—meant that we weren't considered a threat by the other teams. I was just excited to be at the Paralympics, and if we happened to win a medal, that would be the icing on the cake. I talked a big game, but in reality, I always wondered if I had what it took to compete in sledge hockey internationally.

The competition didn't start off well for us. We lost to Norway, who were the team to beat. It was a tough reminder that any mistake in a single game series can end up in the back of your net, but the loss helped us focus and the veteran players reminded us rookies to stay calm. Our next two games against Great Britain and Italy both started out tense. We wanted to establish our lead and prevent an upset. Once we got a couple of goals in, we settled into the games and knocked both teams out easily. We were in the semifinals and slated to play Germany.

I was a little nervous before our game. At that time, the national team didn't travel a lot, so we didn't know much about the European teams we were competing with, and we needed to win this next game to have a chance at the gold medal. Turns out, we had no reason to worry—we scored goal after goal and knocked Germany out 5–0. The underdogs had made it to the finals.

Once more, we were facing Norway, a team which at that time had some of the best sledge hockey players in the world, including Rolf Pedersen, who had been competing in the Paralympics since I was six years old. He was a veteran, an international legend in sledge hockey. Although I was just a rookie, I was determined to win gold. *You belong here*, I thought. *You can do this.*

That game was a battle from beginning to end, but we stuck with our strategy, and Brad Bowden scored our first goal just three minutes in. I drove Rolf nuts all night and he ended up taking three minor penalties. The less he was on the ice, the better our chances.

At the end of the second period, Rolf was in the penalty box. With him out of the way, Brad drove the net, but two defenders were closing in. He dropped the puck back to me. I had an open net, but did I have enough stick on the puck to get it in? There was only one way to find out. I took a swing, and the puck sailed in. I pointed at Brad. *Great pass!*

This photo was taken right after I scored my goal during the gold medal game against Norway at the Turin Games. I'll never forget the rush of excitement I felt when the puck went in.

All the guys on the ice swarmed me. "We're up 2–0! We could actually win this!"

The thought that we could be bringing home a gold medal gave us all razor-sharp focus.

"Let's keep going!" we told each other. "Don't let up!"

We played our asses off and our goalie, Paul Rosen, was a monster in net, stopping every shot Norway made. In the final minutes of the game, they pulled their goalie, and Billy Bridges took the opportunity to score one more goal for us. The buzzer sounded. We'd done it. We got our gold medal. And the best part was my parents were in the audience looking on the entire time.

During the medal ceremony, the officials also gave us flowers. As I received my medal and my flowers, I caught a glimpse of my mom. She was three rows up from the glass. A volunteer must have been watching me because he took my flowers and ran over to the boards and tossed them up to my mom. I'll never forget the smile on her face when she caught them.

"I am so proud of you, Greg!" she said, hugging me after the ceremony.

My dad was beaming. "You've really proven yourself."

I looked down at my gold medal. "I couldn't have done this without you both pushing me to find the right sport for me." I swallowed hard. "Thank you."

Later, my friends told me that Don Cherry and Ron MacLean showed my goal on *Hockey Night in Canada*. It meant a lot to me to see my sport featured on national television—I knew we had made

My mom and I at the 2006 Turin Paralympics. She's proudly displaying my competitor badge. This moment wouldn't have been possible without her encouraging me to try sledge hockey.

Canada proud. Even now, when I think about the moment they raised our flag and played the national anthem, I get chills.

After Turin, I was on such a high. Before the Paralympics, I thought I might start on the path towards becoming a general manager of an NHL team because that's something that had always interested me. But our victory in Turin inspired me to keep going with sledge hockey.

After I finished my degree, I thought once more about retiring from sledge hockey, but then I was given the tremendous honour of becoming the captain of the national team, and I made it my goal to lead the guys to another gold at Sochi in 2014. We had not done well at the previous Paralympics in Vancouver. We'd finished fourth, which stung, especially because the event was in our own backyard. We realized that the sport was evolving and that we needed to be bigger, faster, and stronger if we were going to compete on the international stage.

We went on to capture bronze in Sochi. Still, bronze was not the standard we'd set for ourselves, and my stubborn streak meant I wasn't giving up another gold medal without a fight.

Heading into the 2018 Paralympics in Pyeongchang, our team was hungry for the chance to dethrone the back-to-back champions, Team USA. Brad, Billy, and I were the only remaining players from the 2006 team. The rest of the guys were a talented group of young players who had fully committed themselves to being the best they could be—if anyone deserved a gold medal, it was them.

These were my fourth games. I knew the tournament, I knew the teams, and I knew we could swing through the preliminary rounds without an issue. On the ice, our strategy never varied—score early and maintain the lead—and our goalies, Corbin Watson and Dominic Larocque, who had been with the team since Sochi, were experts at denying opposing shots. As I predicted, we came out of the gate strong, knocking out Sweden, Italy, and our old rivals, Norway, without letting in a single goal. The best part was that our rookies, Liam Hickey, Dominic Cozzolino, and Rob Armstrong, were racking up the points, scoring and assisting their first, second, and third Paralympic goals. The previous year at the world finals, Rob was a healthy scratch; now he was a top-four defenceman. I was so proud of how far our newest players had come.

In the semifinals, we faced off against Korea, and we continued our shutout streak. We were playing better than we ever had before, but the question on all our minds was if we had what it took to beat the United States. We had been tracking their team's progress throughout the games, and as much as we hated to admit it, they were playing just as well as we were.

In the locker room before the gold-medal game, I took a few moments to address the team.

"When I look around this room, I see incredible strength," I said. "Everyone here chose to go against the grain, to see their physical disability as an opportunity, not a limitation. No matter what happens tonight, we have already fought and won the most important battle." I paused. "But let's give the US a fight they won't soon forget."

"Yeah!" they cheered.

We had momentum right from the start—our defence was strong and Dom was in net. At the end of the first, Ben Delaney had scored, giving us the lead. As we expected, the US amped up their offense, looking to tie the game, but Dom just kept blocking every shot. They kept us busy, too, though, and we struggled to get the puck past their goalie, Steve Cash. As the clock ran down, it looked like we were going to win with just one goal, but we couldn't let up, we couldn't give the US an opening to score.

In the final minute, they pulled their goalie, and Rob took the opportunity to take a shot on the open net, but the puck hit the post.

What happened next was surreal. The U.S. pushed into our zone and their forward Declan Farmer caught a loose puck. Dom stretched to block the net, but the puck sailed high and landed in the top shelf. With just thirty-seven seconds left, they had tied the game. We were going into overtime.

We were a bit quiet as the clock restarted—we went from thinking we had the game in the bag to readying ourselves for the final battle—but we were in a positive state of mind.

"Let's stay aggressive," I said.

Dom, as usual, was calm and ready. Farmer made a beeline for him at the beginning of overtime, but Dom pulled out an incredible save. We tried to force a turnover, but Farmer came right back and shot high over Dom's blocker. The puck went in. In that moment, I think all our hearts broke a little.

After the game, the mood in the dressing room was somber as the game ran through our minds. Should we have done a few plays differently? I was sure Rob wanted that shot again. What if I had stood up at our own blue line more aggressively? Or shadowed one of their players better? I knew I would drive myself crazy if I thought that way, so I focused on the good.

In the last three years, our team had improved so much, and that was because of the talent and dedication of our youngest players. Their hard work inspired me. It was what had brought us to the Paralympics, and it was what would keep us going after.

"This loss feels bad today," I said. "But the truth is our team is playing the best it ever has. We might not have gold today, but there's gold in our future. For now, every one of you should be proud of what you've accomplished here, not just for Canada, but for the sport of sledge hockey."

I was speaking to myself as much as the team. Yes, I still want another gold medal, but what I want has evolved beyond that. Playing sledge hockey for Canada has given me the opportunity to advocate for sports for the disabled. I'm a big believer in getting kids involved in sledge hockey, where they can make friends and stay active. Through my charity work, I've meet some truly inspirational people: kids with disabilities, cancer survivors, and Canadian soldiers who have lost limbs in the line of duty. These are the people who motivate me today.

A few years ago, I was in Edmonton visiting my buddy Matt, who was battling cancer. While I was there, I received a phone call from another friend. I could tell from her voice that something was wrong.

"Greg, my friend Michelle was in a terrible motorcycle accident and she's lost her leg."

"That's terrible. I'm so sorry to hear that."

"I think it would mean a lot to her to meet you. Would you be able to come and see her?" my friend asked.

"Of course!" I replied. *I hope I can help*, I thought as I said goodbye to Matt and jumped in the car.

At the hospital, I met Michelle and her mother. Michelle had almost died, I learned, and had been on life support for a week. As we chatted, she told me that she loved snowboarding and had just recently competed in her first fitness competition. I encouraged her to continue following her dream to become a professional snowboarder and we had a good conversation about living with disabilities. Michelle went on to make a full recovery, and three years later, she competed in the 2014 Paralympics in Sochi, becoming the first woman Canadian Paralympic snowboarder. Michelle Salt is a fighter.

Months later, I was at Holland Bloorview Hospital in Toronto getting a checkup on my legs, when I saw a toddler with the exact same prosthetics as me. I asked the receptionist at the front desk if I could meet the boy's parents. She said yes and pointed them out to me. When I saw them, I couldn't help but think of my own parents, how they had to make that huge decision to have my legs amputated, and how worried they'd been about my quality of life. I know it would have meant the world to my mom back then to hear that her son was going to be okay. I wanted to assure this boy's parents that he was going to walk and live a normal life, just like me. I introduced myself to them and shared a little bit of my story, and the boy's mom started to tear up. "They're tears of joy," she said. She was so relieved to know that everything was going to be okay for her son.

My parents have been instrumental in my journey. They helped me accept the reality of my situation but not be limited by it. They set me free to go after whatever I wanted. I can't imagine where I would be in life without sledge hockey, which is incredible, considering I wasn't sure if I would even like the sport when my mom suggested it all those years ago. I've been able to travel the world and represent my country doing something that I love. Wearing that Team Canada jersey has taken on a deeper meaning for me. Now when I put it on, I am overwhelmed with the sense that there is a whole other team outside of the guys in the dressing room watching over us: the people that support us and our sport. That community spirit is what the jersey means to me today. Life doesn't get much better than that.

Greg Westlake is a Canadian sledge hockey player, the captain of the Canadian national team, and the third all-time scorer in Team Canada history as of 2016. A three-time world champion, he has won three Paralympic medals. He has worked for CBC Sports as an in-field reporter during the Toronto 2015 Parapan American Games and the 2016 Paralympic Games in Rio. He's also a spokesperson for Jumpstart's Play Finds a Way program, which aims to make sport and play accessible to all Canadian children. Follow him on Twitter at @gwestlake12.

Reaching Out

Karina Potvin

The year before, these kids had been in a refugee camp in Lebanon; now they were playing hockey just like so many other kids in Canada.

So much about Canada is welcoming. Well, except maybe our winters, but they're a small price to pay in order to play hockey, a sport I consider to be distinctly ours. I played for Team Ontario's under-eighteen squad and then I was the captain of the University of Ottawa Gee-Gees women's team for two years. I tried out for Team Canada, and at the Ontario selection camp, Cassie Campbell—a future gold medallist—was my roommate, so that was cool. I didn't make it past the camp, but my passion for hockey hasn't let up.

Today, when I'm not teaching high school, you'll find me coaching my son Benoit's Ottawa East Minor Hockey Association Novice team (ages seven to nine) at one of the many rinks of the Bytown Minor Hockey League in the Ottawa area. And most Saturdays you'll find me at home, in front of my TV, watching *Hockey Night in Canada*, and if my hometown team, the Ottawa Senators, is playing, I'm cheering louder than my husband and three kids. What can I say? I love hockey.

After one of these games, the news popped on, and there in front of me was Prime Minister Justin Trudeau greeting Syrian refugees at Pearson airport in Toronto. As I saw those happy faces, I knew I wanted to help these new Canadians feel at home. I just wasn't sure how.

A few months later, I was at a practice when I saw one of my fellow coaches, Allan Martel, coming towards the bench. I could tell he was excited from the spring in his step.

"Karina!" he yelled over the din of kids playing on the ice. "Ted and I have a new idea for Reach Out."

Reach Out is a program in our hockey association that helps low-income families pay for equipment and registration fees so that their kids can join our league, and Ted Ryan is the committee chair.

"Oh, yeah? What is it?" I kept my eye on the kids' skating drills.

"You know how my wife and I have been working with some of the Syrian families who have settled here in Ottawa?"

I nodded. Allan's wife was from Lebanon and spoke Arabic fluently.

"We took a family to one of Fahed's games last week, and their sons absolutely loved it. They had never heard of hockey before, but they want to play."

"Really? That's great. Is Ted going to get them equipment?"

"Oh, he's doing more than that. He's renting a school bus and bringing all the local Syrian refugee families to the rink for public skating. If any of their kids are interested in hockey, he'll get them hooked up with everything they need to play in our league."

I tore my gaze from the action on the ice. "That's amazing! What a good way to get the families involved in our community and allow those kids to be kids. If there's anything you need, just let me know."

"Actually, there is." Allan smiled. "We think we'll need you to coach some of the new players since a lot of them have never skated before. That's your specialty."

"Of course, I'd be happy to." I was just so proud to be part of what Allan and Ted were doing.

"Fantastic. We'll keep you posted."

When I trained to become a coach, I specialized in skating skills and power skating. I was a figure skater before I played hockey, and that sport's focus on edgework to develop the right combination of balance, power, and mobility was something I emphasized when I coached hockey. On top of that, my brother is a highly qualified skating coach, and I picked up a lot from him over the years, so I had the right skills to help the boys on the ice.

But I also knew that coaching wasn't just about explaining how to do a crossover or a tight turn; it was also about connecting to the players as individuals. I'd worked with underprivileged and new immigrant families at the local community centre, and over the years, I'd developed friendships with families of different cultural backgrounds. They'd taught me about the Muslim religion and some of the differences between life in the Middle East and Canada. Thanks to them, I had a better understanding of Middle Eastern culture and didn't feel nervous about relating to and coaching Syrian kids.

That summer, Ted and Allan worked tirelessly to help the Syrian refugees in our community feel welcome. With the support of sponsors like Canadian Tire's Jumpstart program, the Ottawa East Minor Hockey Association's Reach Out outfitted fifteen kids with equipment and registered them to play hockey. That's when I got the call that two brothers, Mohammed and Ahmad al-Masri, and Ismael Yasen would be on my team, the Novice C Coyotes.

I met my new players in the locker room before our first practice of the season. "Hi, my name is Karina. I'll be coaching you this year. Can you tell me your names?"

"I'm Mohammed," the tallest boy said, then spoke for the other two. "And this is my brother, Ahmad, and my friend Ismael."

"Nice to meet you all." I replied. "Are you excited to play hockey?"

"I can't wait," Mohammed said. Ahmad and Ismael smiled and

nodded. I was getting the impression that Mohammed was most outspoken of the three.

"Okay, then let's get out on the ice."

Initially Ted, Allan, and I had been worried that we'd need a lot of help communicating with the Syrian players, so for a few weeks at the start of the season, we had students fluent in Arabic come from Carleton University and stand at the side of the boards. If we needed to relay a messages to the kids during practice, the students would translate. But the kids didn't need a lot of help communicating with us. They already spoke English quite well, and since hockey is such a visual game, anything we coaches demonstrated, the players picked up pretty quickly.

I have to admit, though, during those first few practices, it was clear that Mohammed, Ahmad, and Ismael didn't know what to make of a woman head coach. I don't think they had ever seen one before. At the beginning, they seemed to respond more easily to the male assistant coaches, but they would always point the kids towards me and say, "Coach Karina is the boss, and she makes all the decisions. Talk to her."

Mohammed had so much energy that he often went ahead and did things his own way, which isn't unusual at the Novice level. I'd have to pull him back and slow him down.

"It's not about doing these drills fast, it's about doing them right," I'd remind him.

He was never impolite, just liked to question things, but once he saw that my male counterparts respected my coaching, that I could carry myself on the ice, he began to respond to me. There was never a problem after that.

The boys all rolled their *R*s, so I always knew when it was them calling me. "Coach Karrrrrrrina," Mohammed would shout as he got to the rink, "what are we practicing today?" And once I showed them what they needed to work on they were relentless. They would go to public skating, they would go to outdoor rinks, they would go anywhere to skate in order to get better.

Everything was going really well, until we realized that the parents of our players had to take Speak Out!, a mandatory course on the prevention of bullying, harassment, and abuse in hockey from Hockey Canada. It's a wonderful program, but it's offered only in English, and the parents of our Syrian players were still learning the language. We tried to petition Hockey Eastern Ontario (HEO), a wing of Hockey Canada, to give these refugee families a pass because of the obvious language barrier, but the organization said no. If the parents didn't complete the course, I wouldn't be able to put Mohammed, Ahmad, and Ismael on my official roster.

Cue the wonderful students from Carleton! They volunteered their time and went to the apartments of each family in our league to translate the course for the parents. With their help, the parents completed the program and got a sense of what to expect in Canada. I was thrilled that Mohammed, Ahmad, and Ismael were on my team. And when they stepped onto the ice for that first official game, I was smiling so big that my face hurt.

I remember running into Ted one November day at the arena—he was coaching a peewee team (ages eleven to thirteen) with four Syrian kids on it—and we got to chatting about how driven our newest players were.

"I'm amazed at how quickly Mohammed, Ahmad, and Ismael have gotten the hang of skating," I said. "They're all over the ice!"

"Who would have known that a few months ago they had never skated before?" Ted said, laughing.

"I'm just glad everyone has the proper handed hockey stick now. And that their skates are sharp." At first, the kids hadn't cared about having the right stick or getting their skates sharpened. They just wanted to be on the ice and playing hockey, so the coaching staff and parents on my team made sure to check all three boys' skates and equipment every practice. When needed, a parent would take care of sharpening the skates.

"You know what one of the dads told me the other day?" Ted asked. "Six years earlier his whole family sneaked across the border into Jordan during the night. He had his son under one arm and a gun under the other. Then they spent four years in a refugee camp before coming to Canada."

I shook my head. "I can't believe what they've had to go through to get here."

"Let alone play hockey," Ted added.

He went on to tell me that his neighbour saw one of the boys making ice on the balcony of their tenth-floor apartment. I knew some of the kids were getting up early to skate before school, but skating on a balcony was by far the wildest example of the passion these boys had.

The kids and their families were making Canada their home, and we were helping them out as best we could. We did have a few challenges along the way: most namely, getting the players and their parents to the rink. I was one of the few people on the team who had a van, so I volunteered to drive them to and from the games when they needed a ride. Luckily, the al-Masris and the Yasens lived in the same apartment building, but often Mohammed would call me with fifteen minutes notice and ask, "Coach Karrrrrina, can you come get us?"

I knew the families were learning a lot of new things all at once, but I had to explain that I needed more notice if they needed a ride, that I had to coordinate with my husband and our three kids. We were all new to this—the parents, sponsors, East Ottawa Minor Hockey Association, and, certainly, me—and sometimes it was frustrating. But I could never be upset with the kids—they had escaped a war-torn country and all they wanted to do was play hockey. We were all trying to do our best for them. I was determined to honour my commitment to my players, and in the end we always figured out a way to make it work. And just seeing the smiles on those kids' faces every time we arrived at the rink? That was worth more than money.

Despite the bumps in the road, the kids thrived. They were like hockey sponges. Once we showed them what the game was all about, they fell in love with it. They watched YouTube videos of goals, hockey plays, and any other highlight they could get their hands on. The more they understood the sport, the more they talked about what strategies we should use during our games.

After one game, Mohammed came up to me. "You should load up the top line, Coach Karrrrrina. That way I can score more goals and we'd win more games."

"I have to keep the lines balanced, Mohammed," I reminded him. "Everyone needs to practice their scoring."

They breathed hockey all day, every day. As did their parents. By midseason, the parents were typical Canadian hockey moms

Here are Mohammed, Ahmad, and Ismael decked out in their Ottawa East Hockey Association shirts and hats.

and dads. Even if we didn't have space in the van for everyone, they always found a way to make it to the game. From my spot on the bench, I could see Moammar, Mohammed and Ahmad's dad, and Easen Amam, Ismael's dad, nervously watching the action on the ice, then cheering for their kids whenever our team scored a goal. The best was when they got out their cellphones to take pictures and videos of the boys in action—they were so proud!

Once when I was speaking to Moammar—Mohammed was translating for us—I learned that he was a big soccer player as a youth. He began telling me about his soccer strategies and how he was seeing them play out on the ice, instead of the field.

He smiled. "I wish I could go back to my childhood to play hockey."

Sport is an international language, I thought. *It doesn't matter what you play or where in the world you play it, there's always a way to connect it to hockey in Canada.*

It wasn't just the al-Masris and the Yasens who were learning new things. My family and I were, too, maybe even more so.

"Can you tell me what war looks like?" I heard my son Benoit ask Mohammed, Ahmad, and Ismael one day as we were driving to the rink.

I cringed. In the rearview mirror I could see each boy's face. Usually they chatted about their school day, when they'd last gone skating, or the latest hockey video they found on YouTube. *Did they want to revisit that part of their lives?* I asked myself.

"We weren't really in a war zone," Mohammed answered nonchalantly. "We were in a refugee camp."

"In Lebanon," Ahmad chimed in.

"What was that like?" Benoit asked again.

"There wasn't a lot of room in the camps, but we went to school and played soccer," Mohammed said. "Our parents tried to make things seem as normal as they could."

"I remember Mohammed had to switch from the French school to the Arabic one," Ismael said. "The French teachers were stricter and he was always getting disciplined."

He started laughing as he described all the times Mohammed got in trouble.

My fingers began to relax on the steering wheel. From working at the community centre, I was aware of how hard life can be for people, but hearing the boys talk about their experiences opened my eyes to what it was like to be displaced from your home. I thought about how quickly Mohammed, Ahmad, and Ismael had adapted to their circumstances. *They're so resilient*, I thought. The year before, these kids had been in a refugee camp in Lebanon; now they were playing hockey just like so many other kids in Canada. Whenever I caught myself complaining about something small, I thought about what the al-Masris and the Yasens had gone through, and I remembered how lucky I am to live in Canada.

Keeping things in perspective is important, and I try and use hockey as a way of teaching my players this lesson, too. Because the players in the Novice league are still so young, my coaching philosophy has always been to get them to play as many positions as I can so they have a better perspective of the game. Early on, Mohammed proved to have a natural talent for scoring. And he was eager.

"Coach Karrrrrina, I'm playing forward today, right?" he'd ask me every game.

"I've got you in net this time, buddy."

He let out a big groan. "Why? I have to be up front to get goals."

"Because I want you to practice stopping goals, too."

Mohammed begrudgingly took his place in net to start the game, but halfway through, he wanted nothing more to do with it. "I want to score goals, not save them," he complained during a water break.

I chuckled. I always found Mohammed's grumbling funny. "I'm

trying to teach you to be a complete player like the guys in the NHL and show you that the goalie position is not an easy one and demands respect." Still, I never made him play goalie again.

Another time I had him playing defence, which didn't please him either.

"My dad says I cannot play on D!"

He was so expressive—I had to fight the urge to laugh. "Did you tell your dad that the coach decides what position you play?"

"Yes, but he says I'm your best scorer."

"You are, which is why it's time to learn how to be a good defenceman. You've never tried it before—how do you know you don't like it?"

He didn't seem convinced.

"Do you like soccer?"

"Yes."

"But you decided to try hockey."

"Yes."

"Now which one do you like better?"

He grinned. "Hockey. You know that, Coach Karrrrina."

"See, if you hadn't tried hockey, you would have never known you preferred it to soccer. So tonight you can see if you really prefer forward to defence."

"Okay, but my dad won't like it."

"That's okay. I'll talk to your dad and tell him why."

With the help of a translator, I explained my coaching philosophy to Moammar, and he was fine with it.

Mohammed was so competitive. If he gave up a weak goal or made a mistake that led to one, he would get frustrated. But each disappointment fueled him. He gave the game everything he had, and by the end of the year, he was our top scorer. I didn't even get to surprise him with the news—he already knew all the stats!

This is the 2016–2017 team photo for the Novice C Coyotes.
I'm in the back row, first from the right. Mohammed is in the
second row, third from the left, and my son Benoit, Ahmad, and
Ismael are in the front, second, fifth, and sixth from the left.

Throughout the season, I learned a few words in Arabic from Mohammed, Ahmad, and Ismael. Of course, they taught me a few bad words, but nothing that I could use in a decent conversation. Allan's wife would often give me feedback from the parents, and when she told me how much the al-Masris and Yasens loved having me as their coach, I was flattered. I had never planned on coaching three Syrian refugees, but I consider myself lucky to have been in the right place at the right time and to get to know some of hockey's newest (and probably biggest) enthusiasts. And you know what I discovered? Hockey is an invitation, not just for those new to the game, but for us old sports, too. By coaching those three eager young boys, I got to be a part of something special.

One Arabic word I learned was *hebbak*, which means "I love you." Sometimes when we were on the bench, I would turn to Mohammed and say it. He always gave me a strange look.

"Yeah, I just told you that I love you. Because you're playing really well tonight and listening to us coaches."

He shook his head. "Coach Karrrrrina, you're weird."

"If you ever make the NHL and they ask you who was your first and favourite coach, you have to say Coach Karina."

"Yes, of course." He laughed.

"And if you ever play for the Senators, you have to get me tickets. And when you get a big, fancy car, it will be your turn to give me a ride."

Every time I said this, he would smile and reply, "Yes, yes, yes." Then, "Coach Karrrrrina, you need to load up the top line."

Karina Potvin teaches at the École secondaire publique Louis-Riel and coaches Novice hockey in the Ottawa East Minor Hockey Association. In 2016, she received the Women Leaders in Community Development Award for her outstanding leadership and dedication to improving her school and community. She lives in Ottawa with her husband and three kids.

The Sweet Sounds of Hockey

Wayne St. Denis

Hockey is for everyone.

I wasn't always blind, but I've always loved hockey.

I grew up on the east side of Windsor, Ontario, and I started playing road hockey with my older brothers when I was five years old. Bryan was seventeen and Gary was ten, and they were just as nuts about the sport as I was and needed a target to put in front of the net, even if that target was a small kid.

"Wayne! We need you in net," Bryan called to me from the driveway.

"Just a sec," I replied from the garage, rummaging around the hockey equipment for the ball.

"Bring the ball, will ya?" Gary chimed in. I could hear his stick tapping against the pavement.

"I'm looking!" I knew my brothers couldn't wait to practice their slap shots on me. I didn't mind, but I knew the ball hurt if you got hit in the wrong place.

"Where's the ball?" Gary asked when I emerged with a handful of sponge pucks.

"Couldn't find it." I tossed a puck to Bryan—it landed with a muted thud—tapped both posts, and got in position in front of the net. "Okay, guys, do your worst."

Before I knew it, they were barreling towards me, their sticks scratching on the pavement as they brought the puck closer and closer. One of them wound up and I felt the soft blow of the puck hit my midsection.

"Denied!" I cried. "Just call me Jacques Plante." Plante was my all-time favourite player. I even read his book *On Goaltending* in hopes of improving my skills.

"We'll do no such thing," Bryan replied, pulling the puck back for another shot.

I lunged for a poke-check but missed, and the puck sailed right into the net.

"And the crowd goes wild!" Gary shouted, running around the net.

He was yelling the same phrase two hours later when our mother

At age twelve, posing in my goalie equipment.

called us for dinner. We had completely lost track of time—the sun had gone down while Gary and I imagined ourselves as members of the Toronto Maple Leafs playing against Bryan, a die-hard Habs fan, for the Stanley Cup as crowds of fans cheered us on.

Three years later, I started playing organized hockey at Optimist Park, one of the two local outdoor arenas. It was cold when I got into my gear in the dressing room, and out on the ice, it wasn't any better. Since I was a goalie, I didn't move around as much as the other players, who were chasing the puck around the ice. Standing in that crease, freezing my butt off in the cold, I wondered if I'd made the right choice being in net.

The first time I stepped into an arena, it was to see the Windsor Spitfires play at the Windsor Arena, or the Barn, as it was affectionately called by everyone. It was an ancient wooden structure that resembled—you guessed it—a giant barn. I remember that inside, along the halls, were old pictures and yellowing newspaper clippings of the teams that once played there, including the Detroit Red Wings in their first season when they were known as the Detroit Cougars. I heard stories that, back in the day, they took boats across the Detroit River to play exhibition games. *Wouldn't it be amazing to have my photo on this wall?* I sometimes thought.

I knew I wasn't the best hockey player. I never dreamed of playing in the NHL—I just loved the sport. Despite all of the hours I spent reading Jacques Plante's book, I never did figure out how to play goal like him. I certainly never thought there would come a day when I wouldn't be able to play hockey.

When I was nineteen, I began to have problems with my vision. At first it started with a blurriness in my right eye. I would see the shapes of my teammates on the ice, but I couldn't make out the details on their jerseys, the numbers and names. I couldn't follow the puck. On the way home from a game, I mentioned it to my dad.

"I think I might need glasses."

"What makes you say that?" he asked.

"I'm having trouble seeing things. Everything looks blurry and cloudy to me."

"I'm sure it's nothing to worry about. We'll make an appointment with our eye doctor and get this sorted out."

I let out a breath I didn't realize I'd been holding. *This is nothing a pair of glasses won't fix*, I thought optimistically.

A couple of weeks later, my parents took me to the hospital for an eye exam, and by then, my left eye was also causing me problems, but I was hopeful that I'd be walking out of the hospital with perfect vision.

When the doctor asked me to read out the letters on the chart, I couldn't. It was like looking through a fog—all I could see was the faint shape of the chart. The doctor tried various lens to correct my vision, but nothing was working.

"So, am I getting glasses?" I asked when the doctor came back into the exam room. I was eager to get back out on the ice.

"Well, no. At least not today." He sat down across from us. "Wayne, it's clear that you're experiencing a significant amount of vision loss, but it doesn't appear to be a simple case of nearsightedness. If it was, we would prescribe you corrective glasses."

"Do you know what's causing the blurriness?" my mom asked.

"Not yet, but my guess is that it's a genetic issue. Is there a history of vision loss in the family?"

My parents looked at each other, and I knew they were thinking of my older brothers Bryan and Gary.

If this was caused by a genetic disease, they would be at risk, too. My dad finally spoke. "No, none that we know of."

"Okay, well, I'd like to send Wayne to London to have more tests done. In the meantime, perhaps you could do some digging in your family history for clues."

"Definitely," my mom said, rising from her seat. "Thank you."

Back in the car, my parents reassured me that we would figure this out, and that everything would be okay. But as I looked out the window at the stream of cloudy shapes going by, I had the unsettling feeling that my life was about to change.

Over the next year, I went for a battery of tests in Windsor, London, and Toronto, as my doctors tried to isolate what was causing my blurry vision. Meanwhile, my eyesight worsened. It wasn't just objects in the distance that were murky; the doctors' faces peering over mine were also foggy. I felt completely alone, like no one else really understood what I was going through. Heck, I didn't even know what was happening to me. The world I knew was gone. Everything was just blurry and foggy.

The doctors suspected I had Leber hereditary optic neuropathy (LHON), an inherited form of vision loss caused by the deterioration of the nerve that connects the eye to the brain. My parents reached out to our extended family, and eventually they discovered a cousin in my mother's family who had suddenly lost his vision in his twenties. He was now deceased, but his family described his symptoms and they matched mine. For the doctors, this relative was a good sign that they'd found the right diagnosis, and a year after my first appointment, I went to Toronto for a test that would confirm their suspicions.

I remember the specialist sitting me down to tell me the results. "Wayne, we've confirmed that you have LHON."

"What does that mean?" I asked.

"It means there's nothing more we can do. You're considered legally blind and will be for the rest of your life. I'm sorry."

My heart dropped to the floor. For the last year, I had held out hope that my vision could be corrected, that I could get back to my life before the moment my teammates became those blurry shapes on the ice. But that hope deflated like a balloon. *What am I going to do with my life?* And then a horrible thought, unbidden, popped into my mind. *I'm never going to play hockey again.*

For months these dark thoughts plagued me, and it wasn't just me. Shortly after my diagnosis, my brother Gary began experiencing vision problems.

"Do you think it's LHON?" he asked me over the phone.

"I don't know what else it could be, Gary," I replied. "I'm sorry. I know exactly what you're going through."

He received an official diagnosis not long after—now that the doctors knew what to look for, there wasn't as much guesswork. Gary moved back home to Windsor to be with the family as both he and I came to terms with our new reality.

With the help of the good people at the Canadian National Institute for the Blind (CNIB), we learned that we could still have a good life and live independently and travel safely. So even though our surroundings became hazy, we could still get around on our own.

Gary and I can still enjoy *Hockey Night in Canada* every Saturday, too—we just have to be really close to the TV and then we can make out certain shapes. After I received my official diagnosis, one of the first things I bought for myself was a beanbag chair, and I set it up right in front of the TV. Between the incredible voices and imagination of commentators like Danny Gallivan and Bob Cole, I knew exactly what was happening on the ice, even if Wayne Gretzky looked like he was skating in a fog. As I realized I didn't need to be able to see to enjoy the game, my outlook drastically improved.

A few years later, I moved to Toronto to study information technology at a government-funded program for those with disabilities, and when I was finished, I found work as a technical support analyst at a national bank. That's when I heard about the Toronto Ice Owls, the first blind hockey team in the world. I couldn't believe it—how did they play? And would I be able to? I hadn't been on a rink in years. I was nervous to check it out, but my love of the game prevailed and I decided to give it a try. I'll never forget walking into the McGregor Park Arena that first time.

"You must be Wayne!" a friendly voice called out, and I saw a shape coming towards me. "I'm Ed Parenteau, manager of the Ice Owls."

"Hi Ed, it's nice to meet you."

"We're so glad you're here. Come on down to the dressing room and meet the rest of the boys."

As I followed Ed down the hallway, he explained the most important difference in playing blind hockey: the puck.

"We need a puck that makes noise so we can hear where it is on the ice, but no one's perfected the right kind of puck yet, so we use a plastic wheel that you would find on a kid's wagon and we fill it with piano pins."

"What about when the puck is stationary?" I asked.

"Yeah, that's the challenge. The sound of the puck is everything for us. Hopefully, soon someone will figure out how to make a puck that's audible even when it's not moving."

We entered the locker room and Ed introduced me to the other players, then outlined how the teams worked. "Each team is made up of players with various levels of visual impairment: the forwards have ten percent of their vision, the defencemen, five percent, and the goalies are almost totally blind. How would you classify your vision?"

"I've got about five percent in my left eye and a bit less in my right. I can see movement on the ice, but it's like playing in a fog."

"Okay, then I think we'll get you playing defence today."

"Sounds good to me," I said, as I laced up my skates. I'd always played goal, but I liked the thought of playing out. *A new position for a new sport*, I thought.

Out on the rink, I took a deep breath, inhaling that damp smell all arenas seem to have. I stepped out onto the ice, and in an instant, all my memories of playing hockey as a kid came rushing back. As we got into position for a face-off, I was much more aware of the sounds of skates digging into the ice than when I was a teenager; the familiarity was comforting. I wasn't sure quite how this was going to go, but being back on the ice with my gear on, about to play hockey, was the greatest feeling I'd ever had.

And then, just like that, the puck dropped, and we started

Here I am forty-four years later in my twenty-first season with the Toronto Ice Owls Blind Hockey Team. In front of me is the metal puck used in our sport.

playing. Thanks to all the years I played hockey, skating was easy, almost like riding a bike. The biggest adjustment was the puck, but as we played, I moved instinctually towards the metallic sound of the wheel careening off the boards. When I felt the weight of the puck on my stick, I realized how much I had missed the game, missed the competition. Before I knew it, I had a good sweat going.

"That was incredible," I said to Ed when we were back in the locker room.

"It is, isn't it? I remember the first time I played hockey with the Ice Owls. It made me realize I could still do anything I wanted." He laughed. "And so can you. Congrats and welcome to the team, Wayne."

"You know, I never thought I'd play hockey again. This is like winning the lottery." I'm sure Ed could hear the happy relief in my voice. "I can't wait to tell my brother Gary about this."

When I joined the Toronto Ice Owls, there weren't many other blind hockey teams. I credit the grassroots work of the Canadian Blind Hockey Association and Courage Canada, an organization founded by fellow Ice Owl Mark DeMontis, for changing that. Mark grew up playing hockey and was on the cusp of a competitive career when he lost his eyesight to LHON. He was seventeen. In 2009, he started Courage Canada to raise awareness for blind hockey and give kids and adults the opportunity to participate in Canada's game.

Over the next three years, players from the Toronto Ice Owls, myself included, met with players on the Montreal Hiboux and the Vancouver Eclipse blind hockey teams to create a unified set of rules. And in 2013, we brought blind and visually impaired hockey players from across Canada to the Mattamy Athletic Centre at the old Maple Leaf Gardens for the first-ever National Blind Hockey Tournament.

To make the tournament more competitive, all the players were divided into four teams based on skill sets.

The atmosphere at the rink was incredible. When I skated out onto that rink for the first time, I was transported back to that moment when the doctor told me I was legally blind, when I thought I would never play hockey again. And there I was, about to compete at Maple Leaf Gardens. It was a dream come true, but the best part was that I was playing with my brother Gary, whom I had invited to Toronto for the tournament. Because of our age difference, we had never played on the same team growing up—although that hadn't stopped him and Bryan from practicing their slap shots on me out in the driveway—but he was here now.

From the face-off to the final buzzer, the energy on the ice was palpable. The rink was bigger than what we were used to, which opened up the game and forced us to make good use of the entire surface. I even scored a goal.

As my teammates congratulated me in a scrum, I turned to Gary. "What do you think of that shot?"

"You must have learned that from me," he teased, referring to my years watching him aim at me in our driveway.

We won that game, and when I was coming off the ice, a man stopped me.

"That was such a great game," he said. "Really competitive. I lost myself in watching it and forgot that the players were blind."

"That's the ultimate compliment," I replied. "Thank you."

Our team ended up taking home the silver medal, but the highlight of the whole tournament was seeing visually impaired players coming together. Throughout the games, I heard people making plans to meet up afterwards and sharing their stories about living with vision loss. *Wow*, I thought. *These people have so much in common and yet they never would have met without hockey.*

That year, I became general manager of the Toronto Ice Owls, and since then we've participated in five successful national tournaments with players from all over Canada and the United States. The best thing about the tournament is that it keeps growing the sport. At home, we're reaching out to young kids who are visually impaired and starting programs to introduce them to the finer points of the game. Internationally, we've been able to connect with blind hockey teams from Chicago, San Jose, Pittsburgh, Buffalo, and elsewhere. Our message is always the same: Hockey is for everyone. It doesn't matter if you grew up playing hockey or are coming to the game for the first time, you can play. Someday we hope to take organized blind hockey to the Paralympics, or to stage a world tournament. I think we can do it—we're a strong team united by our loss of vision and our love of hockey.

It's been twenty years since I first played with the Toronto Ice Owls, and I'm still playing on the team. And this is what I've learned: there's nothing like the sounds of hockey. There's the crisp swishing of skates, the tapping of sticks, and the clanking of the puck as it glides across the ice, but perhaps the most important sound is that of the team. When I break away with the puck and head for the net, the cheers from my teammates are the loudest thing in the entire arena. There's nothing like those yells. I bet if Don Cherry ever saw us, he would call us a bunch of beauties.

Wayne St. Denis grew up playing hockey with his two older brothers in Windsor, Ontario. He is the general manager of the Toronto Ice Owls and has played on the team since 1997. In 2017, he played in the Beep Baseball World Series with the Toronto Blind Jays. A tireless advocate for sports for those with vision loss, Wayne has sat on the board for Blind Sailing Canada. He lives in Toronto.

A Boy with a Dream

Harnarayan Singh

*Being the only Sikh kid in school was a challenge. Many
of my classmates had never seen or met anyone with a
turban before, but I learned from an early age that I had
something that would always help me fit in: hockey.*

I f you grew up in Alberta during the heyday of the Edmonton Oilers'
rivalry with the Calgary Flames in the eighties, you know that it was
impossible to escape hockey, and that was definitely the case for my
family. All three of my older sisters were fans of the game. Especially
Gurdeep. She and I grew up together, obsessed with Wayne Gretzky,
and we created a shrine to "The Great One" on my bedroom wall.

Like every loyal hockey-loving Canadian family, our TV was constantly switched to the channel showing the hockey game. Although,
in many ways, my upbringing differed from that of other kids in my
town.

My parents emigrated from India, and when they arrived in
Brooks in the sixties, they were the only Sikhs in the southern
Alberta town of three thousand people. Both of my parents were
teachers—my dad taught high school math and my mom was a
substitute—and in their spare time, they taught Sikh history, music,
and the Punjabi language to many in the Sikh community. No matter what the weather, every Friday after school, my parents, my

sister Gurdeep, and I would pile into our red Plymouth Caravelle and make the two-hour drive to Calgary for the weekend in order to attend Sikh events and learn about our heritage. I fondly remember playing the tabla (an East Indian set of drums played with your hands) and the harmonium (a pump organ) along with my friends during those days. And after the Sunday service, I would play ball hockey with the same friends I attended *gurdwara* (Sikh temple) with, until the sun went down. Then my family and I would pile back in the car to drive two hours back to Brooks before the night ended, ensuring we would be ready to go for school on Monday morning. For seventeen years of my life, that was how I spent every single weekend.

While my parents went to great lengths to instill values and traditions in us, they also made sure to show how much they appreciated the opportunities that living in Canada provided. Before I was born, my dad had studied for his PhD at the University of Oregon in Eugene, and my family spent a few summers there. They fell in love with the temperate weather and the natural beauty. But Brooks had a good school system and was the first place to give my dad a job when he came to Canada. Even though my mother often urged him to consider living somewhere else like Oregon that had better weather, Dad was very loyal to the town of Brooks. He and my mother would live there for forty years.

My dad was an all-star when it came to math, but the only numbers I was interested in were on the jerseys of hockey players. I was so obsessed with hockey that I even made a numbers game out of it that I could play during school. I would write down the numbers 0 to 99 and try to write out as many players to the numbers as I could think of. My buddies would often point to a random number.

"Number 16?" I said. "That's Brett Hull of the St. Louis Blues." Then I'd list off all sorts of facts about the player.

"What about number 31?" one of my friends asked.

"Curtis Joseph of the Edmonton Oilers. Didn't you see how he stole the playoff series for his team?!"

"99?"

"That's the easiest one ever! Wayne Gretzky. Centre for the Edmonton Oilers and the best player to ever put on a pair of skates!"

How could I ever forget Gretzky? On our birthdays, my parents would hold a special prayer and make sweet pudding known as *parshaadh*, and on January 26, Gretzky's birthday, I would tell my mom that we had to do the same for him. She was such a good sport that she would do it.

While all of my siblings were on their way to being valedictorians of their respective high school classes, I was focused on increasing my hockey knowledge. But there was also another reason behind my game.

Being the only Sikh kid in school was a challenge. Many of my classmates had never seen or met anyone with a turban before, but I learned from an early age that I had something that would always help me fit in: hockey. Whenever I was worried about being included, I would start talking about the latest trade or game, and everything would be fine. I still have friends from those days at Eastbrook Elementary.

Our living room in Brooks was my play area as a kid, and I let my imagination run wild. When hockey wasn't on, I would watch the Toronto Blue Jays and pretend I was Joe Carter. My mini hockey stick became a make-do baseball bat as I swung at a crumpled ball of aluminum foil. And when I got bored of that, I pretended I was Michael Jordan, using an indoor bouncy ball as my basketball and an opened cardboard box placed on the rocking chair as a net. The floor was always an arena of some kind, and of course I set up my toy cars on a specific area of the floor—that was the parking lot.

When hockey was on the television, I forced each member of my family to play goalie as I ran around with my mini stick commenting on my own plays the entire time. I even made up my own crowd noise for when I scored a goal.

"Can you lower your voice?" one of my sisters would say. "We want to hear what's actually going on in the game!"

Anything I watched on TV, I wanted to imitate, and more often than not, I was watching Ron MacLean on *Hockey Night in Canada*. There is a photo of me as a youngster with a kids' Radio Shack toy microphone, pretending to rehash a game on *Hockey Night in Canada*. When I saw Ron hosting the NHL awards, I was inspired to create my own award shows, one for hockey players and one for

Here I am around the age of five,
pretending to be a hockey commentator
with a kids' microphone and speaker
set my family got me for my birthday.

Sikh musicians. I chose a musician of the month and a player of the month and hosted my own awards night, right in my bedroom.

By the time I got to high school, I knew that I wanted to be a broadcaster, but what I didn't know was if there would ever be a role for me in the industry.

One day, during a visit to our family doctor, who was South Asian, my dad and him began a conversation about what I wanted to do for work when I grew up.

"I want to be a broadcaster," I said. "A hockey broadcaster."

"You're a smart kid, but do you realize how experienced the top anchors are in Canada? Look how many years it took them to get to their position in the industry." My doctor turned to my dad. "Do you really want your son to have to wait that long?" He looked back at me. "There aren't a lot of people on TV that look like you."

Should I be more realistic about my chances? I thought. The entire drive home, I couldn't stop replaying what the doctor had said. *Maybe I should figure out something else to do.*

I was, and still am, the type of person who doesn't really stay quiet. And when we got home that day, my parents noticed that something was on my mind.

"I told your mother what the doctor said, Harnarayan. I know you're bothered by it," my dad said.

My mom chimed in. "We think you should follow your dreams and give broadcasting a shot. If this is your passion, then go for it."

"And if it doesn't work out, you're young enough that you can still switch gears," said my dad.

I was happily surprised, especially knowing how educated my parents and sisters were, and the fact that most South Asian parents at that time wanted their children to go into medicine, engineering, or law. My parents had always been supportive. For example, math wasn't my strong point, and with my dad being the only math teacher at the time in Brooks to teach calculus, I figured I would have no choice but to take the course. But when the time came, he said a line to me that I'll never forget. He didn't mind me not taking calculus because I was "never going to take the derivative of a hockey score." And my mom always had my back, giving me encouragement that only moms can, saying she knew I'd succeed at whatever I put my heart to. Having their blessing to pursue what some considered an unlikely path helped give me enough reassurance that I should give my dreams a shot.

"Thank you, Mom and Dad. Your support means the world to me."

I got my first real taste of broadcasting at the local radio station, Q13. One of my friends, Mark Schultz, reported on the high school's news and sports twice a week, and he asked me to join him.

"I know you're interested in broadcasting, Harnarayan," Mark said. "Why don't you come along with me to the radio station? It'll be fun to do it together."

"Really?! Wow. That'd be amazing! Are you sure they'd be okay with me being a part of it?"

To my astonishment, John Petrie, the manager of the station, thought it was a great idea, too, so Mark and I started reporting on all the sports and events happening at the school. For fun, we used random background music; everything from *Inspector Gadget* to the famous *Rocky* theme song. Eventually the segment even got sponsored, and we had to start reading a little promo at the beginning and end of the report. Our segment became so popular that John increased our time and eventually asked us to do the reports during the summer, too.

"People love what you guys are doing and want to hear what the two of you have to say," he said.

The entire experience at Q13 radio got me thinking. *If a little town like Brooks, which is not very diverse, gave me a chance, maybe I do have a shot of making it in this industry.*

I began to research broadcasting programs. I had heard a lot about Ryerson in Toronto, but I was only seventeen when I graduated from grade twelve, and I just didn't feel ready to be that far away from my family in Brooks. When I heard that Mount Royal University in Calgary—which was much closer to home—offered an internship with The Sports Network (TSN), I knew where I had to go.

I was accepted into the program, and sure enough, during my first year, our teacher announced that TSN was offering an internship. Only a handful of students would be selected from all over Canada. Whoever made the cut would spend a whole semester at the company's Toronto studios, learning firsthand about the industry. As he described the internship, I felt a major seed of doubt grow in my mind. I started thinking that there was no way I would come close to landing an opportunity like that. *I can't be a broadcaster at that level. They're for sure not going to choose me. There's no one there who looks like me.* That voice in my head persisted, and I didn't apply.

Several months passed, and the weekend the application was due, Gurdeep coincidentally asked me what was new. I sighed and quietly murmured a sentence about the TSN internship.

She freaked out. "What do you mean you didn't apply? That's the whole entire reason that you chose to go to Mount Royal!"

"I know. I know. But would I really even get it?"

"Harnarayan, you have to at least apply! When's it due?"

"Monday."

"Harnarayan!"

She was right. And her kick in the butt was just what I needed. Right away, we began filling out all the forms. It was like a marathon—the application was extensive, and I hadn't done a single thing before that weekend. One of the requirements was a full essay on why I wanted to be an intern at TSN.

"Where do I even begin?" I asked Gurdeep.

"With the truth. Where you're from and what your dream is."

I started writing, and with Gurdeep's help, I wrote an essay about a kid from a small town who was obsessed with sports and had dreams of becoming a broadcaster. We finished the application and sent it off. A few months later, I was in disbelief when I found out I'd been chosen for a phone interview with TSN.

"Of course you were!" Gurdeep said excitedly.

I was so nervous for the interview. Right before they called, I turned to my sister. "I might throw up. Can you get a bucket?"

"Are you serious?! Harnarayan!"

Then the phone rang.

"Hello?" I said, mustering all my confidence.

I was then asked about my experience in broadcasting before diving into my sports knowledge—fifty questions about every sport you can imagine: the Kentucky Derby, tennis, football, hockey, and so on. At one point, I remember they even asked me to name a few baseball players from the Milwaukee Brewers roster. I was nervous the whole time, but fortunately, I was paying attention to every sporting event I could and had studied as much as possible. Somehow, someway, I did well enough that I was one of eight students from across Canada chosen to intern at TSN.

"I knew you could do it!" Gurdeep said. "You're going to love it!"

That semester in Toronto was an invaluable experience for me, and I was one of the few students that was hired on full-time after the internship ended. As an editorial assistant, I wrote scripts for Darren Dutchysen, Jennifer Hedger, and Jay Onrait. I was being paid to watch games and write the story of the game, but I was also studying the anchors closely, learning how they delivered those scripts. As much as I loved working behind the scenes, inside I knew I would regret not giving myself a shot to be on the air.

I eventually decided to come back home, as the cost of living by myself in Toronto made it tough and I wanted to be closer to my family. I was fortunate to land a job working as a reporter with CBC Radio in Calgary, where I covered a lot of local news, especially the oil and gas industry, but whenever I could, I pitched hockey stories, and if an opportunity arose to go to the Saddledome—if Sidney Crosby was visiting, for example—I was there. Whatever I was reporting on, there was always a quick turnaround time to get the story done and edited before going on air, and that was one of the key lessons I learned during my first month there.

I remember the first day I saw Kelly Hrudey walk into the CBC building—I was starstruck. Kelly was born in Edmonton, and I had closely followed his career playing in net for the New York Islanders, the LA Kings, and the San Jose Sharks. At that time, Hrudey was an analyst on *Hockey Night in Canada*, but I really had no reason to be intimidated. He was always kind to me and would take time to chat with me whenever he could.

In the meantime, I was honing my skills as a reporter—and after a few years at CBC, I was astonished to have Joel Darling, an executive producer with *Hockey Night in Canada*, call me at my desk.

"Hi, Harnarayan. This is Joel Darling," he said.

I knew immediately who Joel was, but we'd never spoken before.

"Oh, hi, Joel," I said. "What can I do for you?"

"Harnarayan, we're looking to do a Punjabi version of *Hockey Night* for the playoffs. Would you be interested in being a part of that?"

I can't believe this is happening, I thought as I stared at my phone.

As I hung up, I silently thanked the CBC for taking this step towards diversity. I'd always wondered if I had what it took to be a sports broadcaster, and there I was, about to do the commentary for our national sport in my mother tongue. I couldn't help but think of all those weekends my parents drove us from Brooks to Calgary to take part in our Sikh heritage, and all of those nights watching *Hockey Night in Canada* together. Now they would be able to watch hockey in their own language. *They're going to be so excited and proud!*

The first-ever games we called in Punjabi were during the 2008 Stanley Cup final. The experienced Detroit Red Wings were taking on the young but skilled Pittsburgh Penguins. I don't think any of us involved at the time had any idea the history we were about to make. There was intrigue amongst the media and we received a ton of attention. Not only that, but people were watching in high numbers. Initially, the show was just a pilot project, but our ratings were so strong that *Hockey Night in Canada* decided to continue the broadcast the next season and have us call the Saturday-night doubleheaders.

I dove into *Hockey Night Punjabi* with everything I had. Literally. I was told I'd done a good job in the initial broadcasts but that there wasn't any budget to bring me into Toronto from Calgary each weekend. I remember how nerve-racking that conversation was with Joel Darling, but I also remember telling him, "Don't worry. I'll be there."

It just didn't make sense for me to move to Toronto for work on just one day a week. Again, the cost of living and what I'd be earning made it financially impossible. I had to figure something out. So I became a travel expert, keeping meticulous spreadsheets that compared prices for flights and car rentals and tracked all my bookings. I would work all week at CBC Radio in Calgary to help pay for my flights, fly to Toronto on the red-eye on Friday night to call games for *Hockey Night* on Saturday, then head out to Pearson International after we were off the air at one a.m., and spend the next few hours on a bench at the airport, so I could be ready to take the first flight back to Calgary early Sunday morning. Once I landed, I would head to the Sikh temple, where my family would be that day. I felt so blessed and lucky to have gotten to *Hockey Night* that I didn't want to risk losing the opportunity for any reason, so that's just how my schedule was for me in the initial years. It wasn't ideal, but I was making it work.

My parents and family were very supportive. "It doesn't matter if they're paying your travel or not, you have to go for it!" they said. I was working my dream gig, albeit in a totally different way than I had imagined. But I was not ready at all to give up on the dream just because of the financial burden or the crazy schedule. I also knew that if I was ever short on money, my family would come through to make sure that I was able to broadcast *Hockey Night in Canada* in Punjabi, every Saturday night.

I didn't want my superiors to know that I was paying my own way. First, they had already told me that it wasn't in their budget, and second, I didn't want to plant any sort of doubt in anyone's mind that I wouldn't be able to make it. There were some crazy times with bad weather and there were numerous weddings and birthdays that I missed, but I was determined to never miss a game. A couple of seasons in, Kelly Hrudey found out what was I was doing, and after that, things drastically changed for me. Travel was covered and eventually so was my accommodation. That was tremendous financial and emotional relief for me, but it also made me feel like I was *really* part of the *Hockey Night in Canada* team and that the higher-ups had acknowledged and accepted my commitment and role in the show. For a Sikh kid from Brooks, Alberta, those years were definitely hectic, and it all happened at a pretty frenetic pace.

We were starting something brand new, and because no one had ever called ice hockey games in the language of Punjabi, and because we didn't have access to the same amount of resources back then, it didn't take long for me to realize there was extra prep needed to ensure that the broadcasts offered our viewers everything they needed and more. I began to develop my own style of notes and lineups, and

Here I am with my colleagues, from left to right, Randip Janda,
Amrit Gill, Harpreet Pandher, and Bhupinder Hundal.

I would gather as much pregame information as humanly possible to incorporate into the show. Together with my on-set partners, I steadily built a name for ourselves, and our viewership grew with each game. The Canadian Sikh community is over 450,000 strong, and like me, many love hockey not only because it's such an entertaining game, but also because it's a way to connect with our fellow Canadians. The fact that we were bringing Canadians from different backgrounds together was just beautiful.

One thing we quickly learned is that Punjabi and English don't always translate perfectly, but we were so comfortable and confident on the air that with the help of family, friends, and viewers, we created a few new terms for hockey. "Penalty box" became *saja dha daba*, meaning "the box of punishment," and "slap shot" became *chapared* shot—in Punjabi, *chapared* means a slap to the face, but we kept "shot," creating a hybrid. The Punjabi community is a loud and proud bunch. They love to laugh, they love to eat spicy food, and they love their upbeat *bhangra* music. We have always tried to infuse the commentary with as much Punjabi culture as we can. If the players have more energy after an intermission, I sometimes say that they must have had a good cup of chai tea. On occasion, when I announce a big goal in a game, I draw out the scorer's name for a long time, trying to beat out the arena's goal horn. It's what's known as a *heyk* in Punjabi music. Needless to say, we have fun every week.

I was so proud of what we were doing with *Hockey Night Punjabi*. It was the perfect blend of multiculturalism, and it was opening doors for my community to enjoy the game we all love. The show continued to progress on a production level as well. After four years of being based in Toronto, the studio moved to Calgary for a few years, which was great, as it was during the time my wife, Sukhy, and I got married. During the Calgary years, we began incorporating Punjabi poetry and more colloquialisms into our commentary. Eventually the show moved to Vancouver, where, thanks to the support of Rogers Sportsnet and the sponsorship of Chevrolet, the team of broadcasters grew and the production quality increased dramatically. All of a sudden we were able to air full pregame and postgame shows full of highlights and intermission segments featuring entertaining debates from the hockey world.

On May 30, 2016, something special took place, which was the defining moment of my career so far. It was game one of the Stanley Cup final—the Pittsburgh Penguins and the San Jose Sharks were facing off—and I was calling the game in Punjabi. The game was tight—going into the second period, Pittsburgh was up by one, but by the end of the frame, San Jose had tied it up. The game stayed even for most of the third. Pittsburgh kept firing shots, but with no luck.

It looked like they were headed into overtime. You could tell that the atmosphere in the arena was tense. But with less than three minutes left on the clock, Penguins defenceman Kris Letang passed the puck to centreman Nick Bonino, who was standing right in front of the net. Bonino shoveled the puck top corner for the game-winning goal.

Earlier that day, I had made a mistake in my prep work, penning Bonino in for left wing, centre, and right wing. "Bonino-Bonino-Bonino" was written on my notes. And when Bonino scored, that's what I ended up saying, "Bonino, Bonino, Bonino" rapidly, except times ten! Little did I know that the goal call would go viral, not just in Punjabi, but in English, all over the hockey world.

The Penguins went on to win the Stanley Cup that year, and their communications team invited me to the victory parade in Pittsburgh. My colleagues Harpreet Pandher, Randip Janda, and Bhupinder Hundal and I all decided to go, but I don't think we really understood the full impact of that Bonino goal call until we arrived at the airport. Every single TV and radio station in the city was playing the Bonino goal call . . . repeatedly. People were stopping us everywhere and asking for pictures.

Everywhere I turned, I heard, "You're the Bonino guy!" I was in shock the whole time I was there.

The Penguins' media staff had set it up so that we could surprise the players in the dressing room before they went onto the ice for the postseason team picture.

"We haven't told the players you're here, so just walk in!" they said.

It was very quiet before we entered the room. I could see the Stanley Cup, the Prince of Wales Trophy, and Sidney Crosby's Conn Smythe Trophy. The players were getting dressed for their year-end team picture, but the moment we stepped into the room, I started shouting out the Bonino goal call. The players were ecstatic to see us! Sidney Crosby, Marc-André Fleury, and Nick Bonino all came up and shook our hands. I was absolutely blown away that the players, the real stars of the game, were thanking us. *Is this really happening?*

Mike Sullivan, the Penguins' coach, said to me. "I don't know if you know this, but you were such a big part of our Stanley Cup run. We were showing videos of your goal calls to get the players amped up before each game."

"Really? Amazing!" I replied. "It's such an honour to be part of your win!"

In the hallways of the Penguins' arena, we all stood to attention as number 66, Mario Lemieux, came towards us. "Which one of you did the Bonino call?"

A hockey legend was speaking to me. I nodded, and offered my hand, but he pulled me in for a hug.

"You're a part of the Pittsburgh Penguins family and our history. I heard you on the radio this morning. Great job."

That was one of those *wow* moments I will never forget.

Over 400,000 fans lined up to cheer on the Penguins for the parade. At the rally, the team introduced all the players, and right after that, the *Hockey Night Punjabi* team. Naturally I re-created the Bonino goal call for the enthusiastic crowd. As a broadcaster, I am not sure it can get any better than hundreds of thousands of fans cheering for you as you stand in front of a mic.

In the months after that game, I started to realize that the Bonino goal call was helping me create a better rapport with people throughout the league and raising awareness about *Hockey Night Punjabi* and the community of Punjabi hockey fans. After that call, when I walked into NHL dressing rooms, players recognized me.

Recently, when the Chicago Blackhawks were in Calgary, I went to interview some of the players, including their all-star Patrick Kane.

"Hey, how's it going, Harnarayan?" Kane asked, shaking my hand. "We've been watching your stuff. I hope you're calling our game."

I was so humbled to have icons from the game greet me on their own.

Another time, we were walking through a hotel lobby in Los Angeles when we came across the Chicago Blackhawks captain Jonathan Toews talking to a bunch of kids. When Toews saw me, he stepped out of the group to come shake my hand.

"Hey, I saw your story on HBO. I just love what you're doing. Keep it up!"

If this was the end of my story, I would be the happiest man alive, but believe it or not, there was still more to come. In the fall of 2016, a miracle took place, one that I had always hoped for but never thought would actually happen. Scott Moore, the president of Rogers Sportsnet, and Ed Hall, one of the executive producers at the company, asked me if I'd be interested in joining the English side as a host. My very first game was going to be a nationally broadcast, all-Canadian matchup between the Toronto Maple Leafs and the Calgary Flames.

I was absolutely flabbergasted, thrilled, and so, so thankful—and of course, I said yes! Then I immediately called my wife. "Sukhy, you'll never believe what just happened!"

"You sound excited! What's going on?" she asked.

"I'm going to be. . ." I started, but my throat felt tight, and I could barely get the words out. All I could think of was my family's history, how my great-grandfather had come to Canada in the early twentieth century, how my parents stuck it out in Brooks, Alberta, to build a better life for our family. "They've asked me to be on the English side of *Hockey Night in Canada*."

"What?! How?! Oh my goodness! That's amazing!" She was also emotional, excited, and so very proud.

I remember saying, "Isn't it just unbelievable?! We are so lucky and so blessed."

I was determined to represent not only all of us who worked on *Hockey Night Punjabi* but also the entire community as well, so I prepared as much as I possibly could. I was filled with excitement but I was also extremely nervous. But the moment I got to the arena the morning of, the teams, the coaches, the media, and the entire production crew were cheering me on. It wasn't anything I had expected, and it meant a lot.

At the Barclays Center in Brooklyn,
New York, getting set to host a game in
English between the visiting Calgary
Flames and New York Islanders.

Daren Millard was the host that night, and I was waiting rink-side to start my pregame report once he had finished his opening comments.

"Tonight we have a very special guest on our broadcast: Harnarayan Singh," he said.

Wow, I laughed to myself in amazement. *He just said my name, and he pronounced it correctly!*

Daren went on to explain a little bit of my story and the sacrifices I'd made to get where I was that day. As I was listening to him, I was so touched that he and the team had gone out of their way to learn about my story and share it with our viewers. By the time Daren threw it to me, I was almost emotional but managed to thank Daren for his kind words, and then started in on the game.

All this exposure is having a huge effect on the South Asian community, and young people are flooding the minor hockey leagues in places like Brampton, Ontario, and Surrey, British Columbia. The Calgary Flames have done so much to support the Sikh community of hockey fans, too, becoming the first NHL team to ask for a weekly video for their team in Punjabi. It's been fun teaching some of the Flames' players Punjabi hockey terms and having Harvey the Hound attend Calgary's Vaisakhi celebrations. Bhupinder Hundal and Randip Janda, my colleagues at *Hockey Night Punjabi*, organized a South Asian night with the Vancouver Canucks at which the first-ever NHLer of Punjabi descent, Robin Bawa, was honoured. It was such a memorable night for the entire community. At the end of the day, diversity is important, but it's really about the sport and the power it has to bring us all together. We couldn't broadcast *Hockey Night Punjabi* if we weren't all so in love with hockey.

I've now been calling hockey games for over a decade, and the novelty still hasn't worn off. Whenever I pull off a script smoothly or

With Hockey Night in Canada *host, Ron MacLean, at a* Hometown Hockey *event in Ontario. He's someone whose broadcasting prowess and knowledge of the game I've always admired.*

finish an interview, I can't stop myself from doing a fist pump, especially because I know my family and my community are listening.

My mother never missed a game until I had kids—now she's all about her grandchildren, Apaarjeet and Mohun. But my entire family, and especially now the kids, get so excited when I'm on TV.

"Every time they show you, the kids scream, 'Dadda, Dadda!'" my wife told me after a game.

Recently, I was a part of the English broadcast for *Hockey Day in Canada*, and none other than Ron MacLean was throwing over to me. A short while later, Scott Oake did the same. I grew up watching these guys on TV. They're the cream of the crop, and somehow I got a shot to work with them. That's a dream come true, and it wouldn't have been possible without my family, without Brooks, Alberta, or, without hockey . . . Canada's national pastime.

Harnarayan Singh is a Canadian broadcaster and motivational speaker. He is a host and hockey commentator with Hockey Night in Canada, Sportsnet, *and* Flames TV. *In 2017, Harnarayan was awarded the Meritorious Service Award by the Governor General of Canada and was named an ambassador for the NHL's Hockey Is for Everyone initiative. He also serves on the board for HEROS, a charity that provides mentorship to vulnerable youth through hockey. A prominent guest on* Hometown Hockey with Ron MacLean, *he's been profiled in the* New York Times, Maclean's, *and on HBO. Follow him on Twitter at @IceSinghHNIC.*

The Trailblazer

Andi Petrillo

*I was eager to learn the ropes, but what I didn't realize
is that hands-on sports reporting experience wasn't
the only thing I'd learn—I was about to get a crash
course in how to be a woman sports reporter.*

I owe a lot of the success I've had in sports broadcasting to my parents. That, and my love of hockey.

Both of my parents are Italian immigrants, and money was always scarce when they were kids. At eight years old, my father started working at a local cinema in Italy to help out the family. Hoping to escape a life of poverty, he came to Canada as a teenager. My mother's parents felt the same, and when she was just a little girl, they came here to make a better life for their family, although when they first arrived, they struggled and often worked overnight shifts to make ends meet.

My parents met at a nightclub called MoMo's. They both loved to dance, and before settling down into careers—my father as an ironworker and my mother in government—they worked part-time at the club teaching ballroom and Latin dance classes after dinner.

When I was born, they vowed to give me a different childhood than the one they'd had, and because of their hard work, they had the means to do it.

*For my sixth birthday, my parents gave
me a pair of roller skates so I could play
street hockey with the neighborhood kids.*

"You can be anything you want to be, Andi," my mother would
tell me.

They signed me up for every kind of lesson, from music to dance
to soccer. It didn't matter if something was considered a *girl* thing or
a *boy* thing, nothing was off-limits. I was an energetic kid who loved
sports, and I was often playing ball hockey with the neighbourhood
kids. Being an only child, I regaled my family with stories or just
rambled on about things I liked.

"You have the gift of gab," my dad said.

I loved being the centre of attention, and I was—except, that is,
when my parents were watching hockey on TV. Then I was just a
distraction from the game.

"Come watch me practice outside, Dad!" I tapped my stick on the
floor. "I learned how to raise the puck!"

No response. My parents were glued to the game unfolding on
the TV before them. At a commercial break, I tried again.

"I'm over here. Don't you want to see me score a goal?"

"You love playing hockey, Andi," my father replied. "Why don't you want to watch the game with us?"

"It's boring," I whined. "Look at me instead!"

"When I was your age," my mother began, "I didn't know what the big fuss was about hockey either. But my parents, your nonna and nonno, were obsessed with the game. They scrimped and saved until they had enough money to buy a TV so they could watch *Hockey Night in Canada* together every Saturday night."

"They did? Why?"

"Watching the game made them feel at home here in Canada." My father exchanged a glance with my mother. "It makes us feel like we belong, too."

"It's part of our tradition," my mother continued. "Every Saturday, my entire family would squeeze into the living room to watch the Toronto Maple Leafs play. That's Nonno's favourite team."

"What's your favourite team?"

My mother laughed. "The Bruins. My favourite player was Bobby Orr, but I could never bring myself to tell your nonno that I wasn't a Leafs fan."

"I'd rather play," I replied, picking up my stick and heading out the door.

It wasn't until the 1987 World Juniors that I realized how entertaining watching sports on television could be. I was playing in my room with my toys when I heard my dad shouting at the TV. Canada was playing Russia, and, by the sounds of it, a fight had broken out. That wasn't unusual. I'd heard my dad get riled up about games before.

"They shut the lights off!" he shouted. "They shut them off!"

I rushed into the room to see what the heck was going on, but all I saw was a dark TV. *What was my dad going on about?* Then the lights slowly began to flicker back on, and I saw players brawling in groups all over the ice. Equipment was scattered everywhere and the benches were totally empty. Everyone was on the ice. The refs were doing their best to corral the players, and as they got them under control, the commentators announced that the International Ice Hockey Federation had declared the game void. Both teams were ejected from the tournament.

"No!" my dad cried. "We were going to get a medal!"

Wow, I thought. *Hockey is a pretty cool sport.*

From then on, I was hooked, and every Saturday you could find me watching *Hockey Night in Canada* with my dad. The funny this is, I don't recall ever wishing that I was calling the game. I didn't even consider broadcasting as a potential career until high school, and even then, I preferred the idea of investigative journalism. I often fantasized about being a famous war correspondent or working on

Here I am in the edit suite at City TV after an exciting day of shadowing Laura Di Battista. After that, I wanted to get into television broadcasting.

in-depth news shows like *The Fifth Estate* or *W5*. I loved the idea of giving a platform to people who otherwise didn't have a voice, of telling their story.

As always, my parents supported my dreams. When I was fourteen years old, my mom, who was working in politics at that time, arranged for me to shadow City-TV's Laura DiBattista. We made our way around the city grabbing interviews and supporting shots before heading back to the newsroom, where the energy was chaotic. When it was time to go live, a calm descended over the place. I was in awe of everything. I wanted a job where I, too, was always on the go and meeting new people. A few years later, I met Libby Znaimer, who also worked for City-TV as a City Pulse reporter. Both women showed me how to put a story together and taught me that the best thing I could do as a reporter was to not have an opinion. Instead, I should just tell the story. They also told me to eat whenever I could because the days are long. They were great role models, and now I always make sure I have a protein bar on me.

After I graduated from high school, I signed up for the media studies/journalism program at York University and Seneca College, and I started volunteering at Rogers Cable, covering all kinds of stories, from news to sports. But I soon discovered that the realities of being a news reporter were a lot different from my teenage fantasies. One week I covered a murder; the next, I had to investigate a suspected suicide of a woman. Heavy stories like these began to weigh me down.

Everything came to a head one weekend when I was riding with a cameraman to a lacrosse game we had been assigned to cover. We were driving on the highway, making good time, when a car crashed in front of us and burst into flames.

"We need to do something!" I said as we slammed on the brakes.

"You're right," he said, pulling over on the side of the road.

I jumped out of the car and looked back at the traffic, waiting for an opening to cross the highway. I started walking towards the car when my cameraman grabbed me.

"What are you doing?" he yelled. "You're going to get in the way of my shot!"

"What are you talking about? We have to help those people."

He held me back. "Are you kidding me? We're first on the scene. This footage is going to be awesome!"

Even though other motorists quickly stopped to help, I was aghast. *How was the news more important than people's lives?* I decided that would be the end of my career as a news reporter; from then on, I shifted my focus to sports broadcasting.

In 2004, I began working for Rogers Cable as a full-time paid sports producer and host. But I knew if I wanted to make it in the industry, I had to look beyond the walls of the station, and after a couple of years I started sending out demo tapes to a number of sports shows.

Anthony Cicione, the VP of *The Score*, flat-out told me that I was overqualified to be one of the voices on the sports-highlight show. I applied to Global Sports, but they ended up giving the job to someone else. It was discouraging to say the least, so when Sportsnet called me about their 6 p.m. anchor position, I was thrilled. This was an incredible chance. I did my audition with Darren Dreger, who at that time was the host of *Hockey Central*. His was a face I saw often on the TV, so I was a tad starstruck, to say the least. But I felt it went well.

After the audition, the senior producer, Jeff MacDonald, pulled me aside. "Listen, Andi, I'm a big fan of your work."

"Thank you." I smiled, but I sensed there was a caveat coming.

"But you're still raw, Andi, and we feel you're a tad underqualified for this position. We don't want to feed you to the wolves if you're not ready."

I nodded. I understood what he was saying, but I was still disappointed.

"Don't worry," Jeff continued. "You'll find something. In the meantime, I'll have my eye on you. Whenever I find a position for you, I'll make sure you get it."

"Thanks, Jeff. I appreciate that." I shook his hand congenially, but I left without giving his promise a second thought. I was sure it was all talk.

At this point, I had been turned down for being overqualified for one job, and underqualified for another. It was frustrating to be stuck in the middle. I focused on my job search and gave myself until the end of the summer to land a sports job. If I didn't find something by then, I was going to leave the industry altogether.

Towards the end of August, I got a call from a former colleague who told me that Leafs TV, a specialty channel owned by Maple Leafs Sports and Entertainment (MLSE), was looking to hire a reporter to cover the Toronto Marlies.

"You should get your demo tape in, Andi," he said.

"I will. Thanks for the heads-up."

This is it—my last shot, I thought as I drove to the MLSE offices in downtown Toronto to drop off my demo.

A few days later, I called to follow up and managed to get Dean Bender, the creative director, on the phone.

"Sorry, Andi, we never received your demo," he said.

"What?" This was my worst nightmare.

"Let me see if I can find it."

I hung up the phone, replaying the day I handed in my demo. *Did I give it to the wrong person?* I wondered.

Fifteen minutes later, Dean called me back. "I have good news and bad news," he said. "Good news is I found your demo tape. The bad news is that we've already filled the position."

"Oh," I said. Why did he bother looking for my tape then?

"I'm kidding, Andi!" he said, laughing. "I just watched it—come in for an audition."

"Great. Okay, I will." I felt like I had been through the wringer, but I was grateful I still had a chance.

I went in for an audition, which was when I found out that the job wasn't for the Marlies, it was for the Toronto Maple Leafs. The stakes had just gotten higher. My audition went well, and four hours later, Dean called me and offered me the job.

I couldn't believe it. I had been mere days away from leaving the business altogether and now I was reporter for Leafs TV.

I immediately told my parents the good news. "It's a two-year contract, but a step up from anything I've done before."

My parents glanced at each other. "We're so happy for you, Andi," my mom said. "But are you sure this is the right decision?"

"You'll be leaving a full-time job with benefits, vacation time, and a pension plan," my dad said. "We're just worried that you won't have job security."

I understood why they were concerned. They'd come from Italy with nothing. All they wanted for me was to be financially stable.

"I know it sounds like a risk," I replied. "But in journalism, there's a lot more freelance work, and this position will look really good on my résumé and open doors for me."

"Of course." My mom nodded. "We support your choice, Andi."

"We're very proud of you," my dad added.

"Thank you. You'll see, this is just the start."

It was my first big break. At Leafs TV, I would be traveling with the team and the rest of the Leafs' media, pulling together stories, and reporting rink-side at games. I was eager to learn the ropes, but what I didn't realize is that hands-on sports reporting experience wasn't the only thing I'd learn—I was about to get a crash course in how to be a *woman* sports reporter.

At first, I was a little oblivious to the sexist comments around me. Not because I was purposely trying to ignore any sexism, I had just been brought up in a household where I was always told that I could do anything I wanted to do.

"Andi, we're sure you're going to be great on the road," one of my superiors told me shortly after I was hired. "We're thrilled you're part of the team."

"Thanks, I can't wait to get started."

"We do want to caution you about the optics."

"What do you mean?"

"If you're ever in a restaurant or a bar and a player happens to walk in, you should leave."

"But what if I'm in the middle of dinner?"

He hedged a bit more. "I've seen a lot of good women in this industry leave because of things people have said about them. And I don't want that to happen to you."

I realized that my bosses were worried about the rumours that might arise if any of the male players was seen talking to me. I knew they thought they were giving me good advice, that they were protecting me from unwanted talk, but I found the whole thing confusing. *What were people saying about these women that was so bad they wanted to leave the industry?* I didn't know, but I determined that I wouldn't give people anything to speculate about and I wouldn't be intimidated.

We hit the road, and as the season went on, I started to see how women reporters were treated differently.

There was one player who really liked to chat with the media. He genuinely took an interest in our lives, and after practice, we would always make a point to say hello to each other. Sometimes I would be on my own, other times I would be with my coworkers, and we'd all talk about small stuff as a group.

This had been going on for a while when a woman reporter came up to me at a practice and asked me if I was sleeping with him.

I was stunned. "What the hell are you talking about? Why would you ever think something like that?"

"I heard that you talk to him after every practice."

"That doesn't mean we're sleeping together," I said. "There's nothing going on."

The experience shook me. Sometimes I would be speaking with a player in a dressing room, and I would start to get an uneasy feeling in my stomach about how it looked that I was talking to a player away from the scrum. *Do they think I'm flirting?* I'd wonder. *I'm just doing my job and getting the inside scoop.*

I was never worried about what the players thought. A lot of the athletes were my age or younger and they were used to being interviewed by women. It wasn't unusual for them to see a woman in the dressing room, and so they never gave me a hard time. It was usually other people around the team, mainly reporters, who made these assumptions, and they started to get to me. About halfway through the season, I was feeling discouraged about the industry. We were on one of our longer Florida road trips and we had a day off between games, so a group of us decided to go to the beach.

I looked out at the water and thought about my career. Was there a place for me here? I felt like everything I did was distracting from my work, just because I was a woman.

We weren't at the beach for too long when Joe Bowen, the longtime voice of the Maple Leafs, stood up and turned to me. "I am going for a walk. Andi, you're coming with me."

"Okay, Bonesy," I said, and off we went.

"Andi, I just want you to know that you are doing an incredible job," he said once we were out of earshot of the rest. "I know this job isn't easy, especially if you're a woman."

"It's pretty tough," I agreed.

"You're doing an exceptional job. Don't let anybody get in your way or get you down." He went on to give me some examples of other reporters in the industry, describing how some of them let little things get to them or how they got too big for themselves.

As he was talking, I felt a huge weight lifting off me. "Thanks, Joe. I needed to hear that."

"If you ever have any questions, Andi, you know where to find me."

That is Joe Bowen in a nutshell. He always had a knack of finding the right moment to say the right thing.

It wasn't long before I took Joe up on his offer and went to him with a problem. It was the beginning of February, and I had just received an email from my boss asking me to work on the four-teenth. At the time, I was in a relationship—and I cared about hokey occasions like Valentine's Day—so I called my boyfriend, who suggested that I just tell my boss that I couldn't work that night. I was already pissed about having to work, but I didn't like my boyfriend's response either. I left my room and went to the hotel gym to clear my mind with a good workout. That's when I ran into Bonesy.

"What's going on, Andi? You seem upset."

"Oh, it's nothing. It's embarrassing."

"You can tell me."

As I explained the situation to him, I expected him to laugh, but he didn't.

"Let me ask you something," he said seriously. "Does Valentine's Day happen every year?"

I nodded.

"And does the opportunity to show your bosses that you're serious about your work come around often?"

I shook my head no.

"Then I think you know what to do. You're only struggling with the situation right now because someone else wants your time. This industry doesn't always care about holidays. Find someone in your life who's okay with that."

"You're right. Thanks."

I ended up working on February 14, and the boyfriend didn't stick around very long, anyway.

When I met hockey legend Bobby Orr, I told him he was my mom's and my two aunts' favourite player. He asked for their names and then he mailed me three autographed photos for them.

If it wasn't for Joe, I don't think I would have made it through that first year at Leafs TV. He was an invaluable mentor to me, and I found myself spending more time with him and his cohost Jim Ralph. I loved to sit between them as they called the games—it was like having my own personal play-by-play and colour commentators. Their energy was infectious, and they taught me a lot about sports broadcasting.

Even though there were hurdles to overcome in the workplace, MLSE provided me with some amazing opportunities, and to my parents' relief, they renewed my contract. I was determined to develop my versatility as a sports broadcaster, and when the chance came to cover Toronto Raptors and Toronto FC games, I was all in. *There isn't anything I can't do*, I told myself.

After four years at Leafs TV, Trevor Pilling, the executive producer of CBC's *Hockey Night in Canada*, asked me if I was interested in doing some sideline work covering ten Montreal Canadiens games. Other MLSE analysts had side work at other networks, so I asked to amend my contract so I could, too, but MLSE said no. It's true that I was also hosting soccer and basketball for them, and that may have been the difference, but I was crushed. I loved my job with MLSE, but I wanted to expand my repertoire. Still, the gig at *Hockey Night* wasn't enough for me to leave MLSE, so I turned down Trevor's offer.

A year later, in 2011, he called me again. This time, it was to come in and audition for a new show called *Game Day*, an hour-long pregame show that was concerned more with feature stories than with the Xs and Os of the game. I would be cohosting with P. J. Stock.

It had always been a dream of mine to work at *Hockey Night in Canada*, a show that had been such a central part of my family for years, a show that had made my grandparents and parents feel at home here in Canada. And if I got the job, I would be the fifth woman to ever work on the show—I would be joining an exclusive group, and the prospect appealed to me. It was an exclusive contract, which meant I would have to leave MLSE. By then, I felt that I had learned all I could from MLSE and I wanted to spread my wings at a new position. I went in for an audition confident that if Trevor was calling me, I had a good chance of getting the job.

I mentioned the opportunity to my good friend Wade Belak, who was working with CBC on the upcoming *Battle of the Blades*. I had met Wade when he played for the Leafs in 2006, and we had become fast friends—we had the same sense of humour, but we could also talk about serious issues as well. It was Wade who gave me my first glimpse into how stressful fighting is in the NHL. As an enforcer, he was expected to play rough, but it was difficult for him to get into that frame of mind, and he would often dread the night before a game.

"Let's plan a lunch and I can introduce you to my contacts at CBC," Wade said.

"That would be great!" I replied.

We scheduled the meeting, but I ended up postponing a day. My nonno was in and out of the hospital and I was too exhausted to go to the meeting. I texted Wade and told him I'd see him at lunch the next day. First I stopped by the hospital to see my nonno, and while I was there, my agent called me with the good news that *Hockey Night* wanted me for the job.

"I got it!" I told everyone in the room. "*Hockey Night in Canada* is offering me the job!"

"Andi, that's amazing!" my parents said.

My nonno couldn't believe it. "My nipotina is going to be on the show I've been watching for decades," he said. "I'm so proud of you."

But it was a bittersweet moment. Within minutes, I received a call from a fellow reporter telling me that Wade had been found dead. All my excitement about *Hockey Night* vanished as the news that I had lost one of my best friends sunk in. *How could he be gone, just like that?*

I was crushed by Wade's death. I also knew my nonno didn't have long and I wanted to make him proud, so I threw myself into finishing up my contract with MLSE and starting my new job with *Hockey Night in Canada*. For the first three months of the 2011–2012 season, I had so much on my mind, I wasn't able to be truly in the moment, which is why when people ask me how it felt to be on *Hockey Night in Canada* that first night, I can't really tell them. I was so focused on doing a good job that the whole night was a big blur. I do remember the moment when it hit me that I was on the nation's hockey broadcast.

It was a few months later, a typical Saturday night at the Air Canada Centre. I was doing the ice-level reporting, and as the lights dimmed in the arena, through my earpiece, I heard the famous opening to *Hockey Night in Canada*. *Oh my god*, I thought. *I'm on Hockey Night in Canada. Everyone will see me. My family will see me.* My knees started to buckle.

"Over to you, Andi," Ron MacLean's voice buzzed in my ear. "What's happening on the ice?"

For a split second, I froze. *I can't believe this is my life*, I thought, then I snapped out of it and started my segment.

Reporting for *Hockey Night* was a dream come true, but the highlight of the whole experience was that before my nonno passed away, he watched me in action every chance he could. I knew I wouldn't be where I was if not for his decision to come to Canada, and I felt like in some small way, I had given him something in return.

A year later, when *Game Day* was cancelled, I took over hosting the iDesk in the studio, anchoring a segment that parcels what plays the fans are talking about online and highlights the main events.

Goalie equipment was brought on our Hockey Night in Canada *set to help break down plays during intermissions. I decided to have a little fun and show off my butterfly technique—or lack thereof!*

What I didn't realize is that by hosting the segment, I had become the first woman to work in the *Hockey Night in Canada* studio on a full-time basis. I found that out when I read the CBC press release. The news didn't really change anything for me. Of course, I was proud to break that barrier for women sportscasters, but at *Hockey Night*, I'd never felt different or singled out for being the only woman on the show—I'd always felt that I was meant to be there on that set, and my promotion was because of my hard work, not my gender.

In early 2016, I got a phone call from Jeff MacDonald, the guy who'd turned me down from Sportsnet ten years earlier. I had a number of broadcasting gigs under my belt since my first audition for Jeff all those years ago—Leafs TV and *Hockey Night*, of course, but I'd also reported on the 2014 Winter Olympics in Sochi, Russia, the 2014 FIFA World Cup, and *NHL Tonight*. Jeff was now the program director at TSN Radio 1050 Toronto, and, true to his word, he had a job for me.

He got straight to the point. "Andi, I want you to host our daily show *Leafs Lunch*."

"Oh, wow, Jeff, that's a nice offer," I said. "To tell you the truth, I never considered sports radio as an option."

"You've built up an amazing amount of credibility in sports television."

"But sports radio is a different beast altogether. I'd be opening myself up to the same kind of criticisms I faced at the beginning of my career. I'm not sure I'm ready to do that."

"I have faith that you are strong enough to handle anything that comes your way." He paused. "And more important, I have faith you can carry on a sports conversation."

I knew what he was talking about. As a TV host, I was the set-up person for the analyst with the expertise. On the radio, well. "I'll have to share my own opinion." I said.

"For two hours a day, five days a week."

Talking about sports for two hours? I could hear my parents' voices: *You've got the gift of the gab.* The prospect of a new challenge in my career *was* exciting. I knew I needed to say yes.

"Okay, Jeff, I'll do it."

"Fantastic, I knew you'd be up for it! You're a trailblazer, Andi."

"What do you mean?"

"You'll be the first woman to have her own daily talk show on sports radio in Canada."

"Are you serious?"

"Yep. You'll do great."

I was nervous, but I approached the show with an open mind, ready to learn and let my passion for the game and the industry shine through, and I think it does. One of my favourite things to do is to talk about sports, so I set up my show to mirror a group of friends sitting around doing just that. I've found that there is a real fear in this industry—and in life in general—of showing vulnerability, but I'm determined to be honest about what I know, and what I don't. I have enough experience to be half an expert, but I'm also half a fan, just like my listeners, so I make a point to ask questions that they want to know the answers to.

I have so much fun every day. And getting to work with seasoned professionals like Gord Miller and Craig Button has made me a better host. I like it when they tease me because it tells me they see me as one of their equals. I like it when they call me out on any mistakes, too. I don't want to be treated any differently just because I am a woman.

Since I started with *Leafs Lunch*, players in Canada and the United States have told me they listen in while they're driving around in their cars. Dave Poulin, my cohost, was doing some work with his former team, the Philadelphia Flyers, and all the guys who work in the rink told him, "Say hello to Andi!" Apparently, the guys listen to my show on their lunch hour. All they hear is Eagles and Phillies talk on their local stations, and they are desperate for updates about the Flyers and general NHL news. Over 90 percent of my show is focused on the Leafs, and yet staff and fans of these other NHL teams tune in to hear what we have to say. To me, that is a real compliment.

When I look back on my career, I think about all the people who got me to where I am today. If my parents hadn't been so encouraging, always telling me to be open-minded and to try new things and that nothing could hold me back, or hadn't been so engrossed in *Hockey Night in Canada*, I wouldn't have fallen in love with this great sport, or broadcasting, for that matter. And I wouldn't have stayed in the business without the support of people like Joe Bowen,

Jeff MacDonald, and Trevor Pilling. Not everyone is lucky to have such wonderful folks in her life, so I'm determined to do my part by mentoring up-and-coming women sportscasters and supporting the women now in the industry. It's tough for women to break into sportscasting. It's competitive, and I've found that women who make it to the field are intimidated by those who are rising in the ranks and vice versa. We have enough barriers as it is. I have a little saying that I tell people: I'd rather be part of a treasure chest full of gold than be the only token. In other words, I'd rather be surrounded by women talking sports than be the lone woman on a show—I want to be in an industry full of smart women with a gift for gab, just like me.

Andi Petrillo grew up in Maple, Ontario, and started her journalism career at the age of nineteen. She has worked as a reporter for Maple Leaf Sports and Entertainment, ESPN, and the CBC, and as a host for Hockey Night in Canada iDesk. *She was recognized with the 2015 Canadian Screen Award for Best Sports Host in a Sports Program or Series for her work during the CBC's coverage of the Toronto 2015 Pan American Games. Her win in this category made her the first woman to win an award from the Academy of Canadian Cinema & Television for her role as host of a sports program or series. She hosts* Leafs Lunch *on TSN 1050. Follow her on Twitter at @AndiPetrillo and on Instagram at @AndiPetrillo33.*

Life as a Blind and Deaf Hockey Fan

Christian Holmes

*I think I was put on this earth to prove people
wrong and to break the glass barriers that are in
place for people like me in today's society.*

From a very young age, my fueling passion was the game that Canadians love and your parole officer seems to hate: hockey. My old man raised me to be a Leafs fan, and growing up, my favourite players were always the grinders and the tough guys. There was nothing like witnessing Tie Domi go out and beat in the face of anyone who crossed him. The enforcers were badasses to the core. Drunk hecklers loved them, church deacons despised them, and they had to constantly fight and sacrifice to maintain their relevance. That really hit home, as it reminded me of my life and the battles I fought growing up. Because the day I was born, my parents were told I was destined to be a vegetable.

I have a disability called Moebius syndrome, which has left me blind and deaf (not to mention my face being paralyzed, along with half my throat). When I was born, the doctors said that I would never be able to walk, talk, or do anything that "normal people" could do. I saw double, and the only thing I could hear were loud noises such

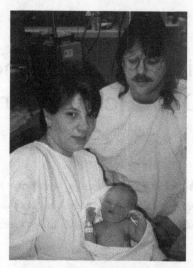

I'm a few days old in this photo.
My mother, Kim, and my father,
Moe, had just been told that I
would never lead a normal life.

as doors slamming or people yelling. Even then I had a hard time making out what people were saying. Forget about watching sports; I could not see the damn game to start off with, but then again, who expects a three-year-old to be able to comprehend hockey anyways? If Columbus was wrong, I may as well have just fallen off the edge of the earth.

I grew up in a small Christian town in Ontario called Fergus. The irony in that is real. Trust me, folks, I know. From the tenderish age of three, my first hero was the Lord. And I don't say that to be a jackass who talks about the big guy upstairs when it benefits my interests. I actually mean it. I wasn't supposed to have the ability to listen to a Metallica album and the wherewithal to grasp what was going on when James Hetfield sang "Sad but True." But thanks to His greatness that wasn't the case. The thing I had going for me was that I could hear, although that ability was supposed to decline as I grew older. After a painful trial-and-error period with hearing aids, I became eligible for something called a bone-anchored hearing device, which used my skull as an eardrum so I could hear somewhat well.

The other thing I had going for me was my mom and her form of bend-back-into-shape therapy. When I was born, I could barely move. I couldn't sit up or lie down on my back or my side. My head bent in an odd manner. My legs were a mess. I was crooked in all senses of the word. I kind of looked like Stephen Hawking minus the IQ. My mom was working for a taxi company and taking care of my two older siblings, Elisha and Devin, but she was determined to do everything she could to help me. With my dad working heavy overtime hours, my mom quit her job and created her own physiotherapy routine that she performed day in, day out until I could sit up straight, walk up and down the stairs, and crawl into my bed. My mom also figured out a way to bottle-feed me by pressing my paralyzed lips together, so that child protective services wouldn't have to have the doctors put a tube in my stomach. By the time I was four, I was able to do all the things a kid my age wanted to do. I could walk, slightly see the forest from the trees, and watch hockey, which is how I found my second hero, longtime NHL tough guy, number 28, Tie Domi.

I'll never forget the first time I watched Tie play. The Leafs were playing the Rangers, and Tie beat the absolute snot out of this sixty-cent player who had taken a cheap shot at Mats Sundin. I instantly realized how integral a player like Domi was to his team. He didn't get the glory of flashier names like Mats Sundin, Ed Belfour, Bryan McCabe, Darcy Tucker, or Gary Roberts, but he fought for every ounce of admiration he received. He was a part of the "brotherhood," and he upheld "the code." By Domi doing what he did, I saw how loud his actions truly were and how respected he was. Later on in the period, Sundin scored and saluted Tie on his way back to the bench. That gave me chills.

I got the chance to meet Tie in person two years later, when I was six. The Leafs had just beaten the Canadiens, thanks to a pair of goals from Matt Stajan. It was surreal. As I entered the locker room, Stajan shook my hand and said hello, and Darcy Tucker stopped by to give me a high five. Then the man of the hour, Tie Domi, came and greeted me. He was wearing a beautiful black suit with a sharp pink tie, and he had a bit of a bruise on his cheek from fighting with a Chris Nilan wannabe. Tie gave me a customized Tie Domi winter

Here I am, decked out in my Maple Leafs jersey, meeting Tie for the first time.

hat (one that I still wear to this very day) and said to me, "I got in a fight for you tonight, buddy!"

I said, "Right on, Tie!"

Tie always had his friends' backs, even mine. When a CBC cameraman called me "ungrateful," because I wasn't smiling—he didn't know that I actually couldn't smile—Tie went up to him and stared him right in the eye and said a few things. The cameraman quickly said sorry to me and ran out of the locker room.

Tie picked me up. "Don't take shit from anyone," he said. "Keep your head up and keep kicking life in the butt. I know you're going to go far."

I was happier than a pig in shit.

So, how do I see hockey games exactly?

Well, I'm legally blind, but thanks to my hefty prescription glasses that have more prisms than a Pink Floyd album cover, I can see a vast majority of the things that others can on TV. I have a hard time tracking the puck when I'm watching hockey, so I use my index finger to help me keep my eyes on it. Yes, it has its downfalls, but for the most part, it works. Especially when I'm watching hockey live. When people ask what the fuck I'm doing, I tell them that I'm following the puck. Before the game, I try to get a sense for the "feel" of what the game will be like. If it feels like it's going to be lacklustre, I'll tend to pay less attention to what's going on in the play and just listen to the game. But if it's one of those crazy games where everything is happening, I try to use my left eye to see what's going on throughout the ice and use my right eye to focus more on the puck.

I have no side vision, and to compensate for that, I'm always moving my head left and right, which people who don't know me find odd. At a Niagara Ice Dogs game, I once had a scout tell me that I pay way more attention to the game than most of his colleagues do.

"Holy shit!" I said. "Really?"

"Yep." He nodded. "What do you think about Ryan Strome?"

"He's overrated. Dougie Hamilton is going to be the better player out of the two."

He rolled his eyes. "I don't think so, kid."

"He's got that right-handed shot and an offensive touch. He's big and strong, too."

He wasn't convinced, but in the end, guys like Brian Burke ended up agreeing with me, and that's all that matters.

As for how I hear hockey, it's a deaf-by-the-kill-switch scenario. When my bone-anchored hearing device (a.k.a. a BAHA) is turned on, it vibrates through my skull and sends sound to my middle ear so I can hear. Technically, I do "hear" voices in my head. Thanks to the recent advances in technology, my current BAHA has Bluetooth capabilities, which means I can literally listen to music on the darn thing, not to mention stream Fan 590 onto it. It really helps me with keeping my eye on the puck. I hear Joe Bowen's vibrations. I listen to him point out the big stuff going on in the game, and then I follow it with my index finger.

My BAHA doesn't compensate for everything, though. I'm still hard of hearing, even when Joe belts, *"Holy mackinaw!"* because the background noises blend in with his voice. That's why I've learned to be very attentive to what's going on and have that other level of awareness when I'm watching games—that "feel" for the game. If I don't have that sixth sense, I end up missing most of the important things, like big battles along the boards, clever little chip outs by the d-men, and stellar back-checks by the forwards.

Now before you give me pity, just remember this: I don't see my disability or any of the complications I face today as a punishment from Satan. I do see it as a gift from Him (or a/the higher power that counselors talk about at the twelve-twelve step AA program). Living with my complications can be hard, but I always say, "It is what it is. Take it or leave it." I'm lucky to be where am I today, because the game has taught me that I don't have to be the biggest or strongest guy to make it farther in life, but I do have to fight for myself. As the old saying goes, "It's not the size of the dog in the fight. It's the size of the fight in the dog." That's a lesson Tie taught me. That's a lesson I'll never forget. As my grandfather used to tell me before he passed, "You just have to be yourself. Not everybody is going to like you, but that's okay. If you like you, that's all that matters." May God bless the man, because the day I forget that teaching is when Hell freezes over. Although, with Nick Foles and the Eagles winning the Super Bowl, some people may argue that's already happened.

I want to be the next Don Cherry and have a cornerstone show that every Canadian needs to tune into on a Saturday night. That involves building credibility in the hockey industry, but I'm willing to put in the hard work. Not to sound condescending or full of my-self, but I think I was put on this earth to prove people wrong and to break the glass barriers that are in place for people like me in the today's society. That's what I believe I am doing now, and that's what I believe I will continue to do as I keeping running back and forth from the bench.

Christian Holmes is a journalism student at Humber College in Toronto. Known as Christian Mingle and Holmesy, he spends most of his time living life, sipping on Budweiser, listening to the Hip, being a smart-ass, and building his writing portfolio. He writes for Grandstand Central *and has been featured in Artifact-News.com and* Last Word on Hockey. *In the future, Holmesy strives to be an NHL exec and report on the Leafs. Follow him on Twitter at @HolmesyWrites.*

Find a Way

*I could have been out cold on an operating table at that
very moment, but instead I was sitting in the back of the
van headed home. While I had a long road to recovery
in front of me, it didn't seem so scary anymore.*

Three seconds was all it took to change my life forever. I was sixteen, starting my rookie year with the Kitchener Rangers in the
Ontario Hockey League (OHL), and my coaches had told me that I
had potential to go far. I believed them, too, until I woke up in the
hospital on November 1, 2009, with no memory of why I was there.

When I opened my eyes, I saw that I was lying in a hospital bed
surrounded by machines and cords everywhere. A doctor's face
came into view.

"Ben, do you know why you're here?" he asked.

"No. What happened? Am I okay?" I started moving my arms and
legs. *Thank god, they work.* That moment of relief was quickly followed by a more frightening thought. *What's wrong with me?*

The doctor's voice broke through my panic. "What's the last thing
you remember, Ben?"

"I . . . I don't know." I paused, concentrating. "I was in Brampton
for a hockey game. I remember walking out of the rink and saying hi
to my parents."

"Anything after that?"

"No." I started to tear up. "What's going on?"

"You were hit from behind on the ice two nights ago. You've suffered a fractured skull, facial lacerations, and you have three separate brain bleeds—two on the surface of your brain and one inside your brain." He paused. "You're lucky to be alive."

All that from one hit? How is that possible? "But I feel fine," I said. "What happens next? When will I be able to get back out on the ice?"

"Ben, I'm afraid that's not going to happen any time soon. This is one of the worst head injuries to sustain. You'll definitely need to take a couple years off from school. I doubt you'll ever play competitive sports again." The doctor went on to explain that I would likely need someone to help care for me for the rest of my life and that I might not feel like my old self ever again.

It was a reality I could not comprehend.

Ever since I was a little kid growing up in Oakville, Ontario, my life had been about sports, all day, every day. My older brother, Chris, was smarter and more naturally athletic than I was, but I tended to work harder at being the best, and as a result we were always extremely competitive, a trait I think we got from our dad. My poor mother would often have to referee us. We couldn't even walk down the hallway without wrestling.

Sports were a great outlet for me. From ages eleven to fourteen, I played hockey, soccer, basketball, volleyball, and lacrosse, and I was on the swim team. My mom still says those four years alone made her go grey.

My teacher would often call my mom at work. "We need Ben for the game tonight, Susan. Do you think you can spare him?"

"I'm not sure. He has an assignment due tomorrow," my mom would say.

Here I am at eight years old playing for the Oakville Rangers AA team. As you can see from the look on my face, I was concentrating hard on defending our zone.

"I'll give him an extra day to get that done so he can come out and play tonight."

"Okay—that works. He'll be there."

While I loved playing all those different sports, hockey stood out from the rest. Whenever I walked into the arena, that smell of the rink hit me and I knew it was going to be a good game, win or lose, because I was going to be with my team and we could face anything together. Even as I moved up in the league, that sense of camaraderie never faded. It's what made me a good hockey player. I wasn't a goal scorer, but as a defenceman, I was skilled at making good passes, and whenever I made a play that allowed a teammate to score a goal, I felt an incredible combination of gratitude and confidence.

Despite my love of the game, playing in the NHL seemed like a far-fetched goal, and so I continued to play soccer and other sports. But all that changed when recruiters started showing interest in me during my Major Bantam year. I was just fourteen, but schools were telling my parents that they were watching my hockey career closely. I realized that if I focused more on my hockey skills, there might be more opportunities to play professionally down the road. I began to spend more time at the gym to increase my strength and speed so that I could provide my team with a strong offensive edge.

The next year, my OHL draft year, I played defence for the Mississauga Senators. On the ice, I was never a tough guy. I didn't run around and try to bodycheck others or punish them in the corners using my body. Instead, I used my hands and my head. I concentrated on being a skilled, smooth-skating defenceman, the kind who could hit a teammate's stick with a pass from half a rink away or rip a perfect slap shot from the point.

I played a strong season with the Senators and people were saying that I was going to be a first-round pick in the OHL draft.

"Not if that means he's moving far away," my mom would say.

She's the boss of all bosses. "Ben, I want you close to home. You can play for Guelph or Kitchener, and if you don't like those options, then I'll let you go to school in the US, provided it's in a state that borders us."

I would nod along—really I was just interested in being a first-round draft pick. I was fifteen and I thought that my entire life depended on what round I was drafted in.

"I'll do some predraft networking," my adviser Rob Hooper said, to my mom's great relief. "I'll make sure Ben ends up close by."

The day of the draft, my mom and I were both nervous for different reasons. When they announced in the third round that the Kitchener Rangers had selected me, she was overjoyed, but as you can imagine, I was upset. I thought my hockey career was over.

Luckily, Rob knew just what to say. "In the long run, what round you're drafted in doesn't matter, Ben. The Kitchener Rangers are a fantastic team and they've got big plans for you."

This is just the beginning, I thought, feeling excited by the new road in front of me.

The Rangers gave me a warm welcome and set me up with Dave and Wendy Brum, an amazing billet family, who put my mom at ease about me moving away and instantly made me feel at home. I wouldn't admit it to my mom, but I was worried I might be homesick. Those fears flew out the window on day one, when Dave and Wendy told me that they had billeted the former Rangers captains Derek Roy and Mike Richards. *This is just the beginning*, I reminded myself.

I got along well with Dave and Wendy. Dave was like my own dad in a lot of ways. As long as I came home in one piece and didn't empty the minifridge, we were good. And Wendy was very forgiving. Not long after I moved in, my teammate Ben Thompson and I forgot some home fries in the oven and left for team yoga. When I came home and saw the look on Wendy's face and the house full of smoke, I thought I was done for, but she was good about it, and we still laugh about the whole incident now.

As the season started, I was determined to prove myself an invaluable player. My coach, Steve Spott, or Spotter, as we called him, often complimented me on my skating in a backhanded manner.

"Nice job making up for that slip on the ice, Fanelli," he'd say. "You're lucky you're a strong skater."

I had done well in the team's under-seventeen training camp, but Spotter and his assistant, Troy Smith, made it clear that we rookies wouldn't be in the lineup for every game.

"We're confident in your abilities," Spotter said. "But you guys are young, and part of my job as a coach is to teach you how to play hockey at this level, so we'll get you on the ice gradually."

I was happy to be on the team. When we played on home ice, the crowds of eight thousand cheering fans gave me such an adrenaline rush, even when I was just sitting on the bench. *I could get used to this*, I thought, and the more time I spent on the ice, the more comfortable I became. I had visions of playing professional hockey for many years. But life had other plans.

When I woke up in the hospital that day and the doctor told me I might never play hockey again, I felt like my world had ended. Everything that I had been striving for was suddenly out of reach. Fortunately, my parents and my brother Chris were right by my side. After an initial checkup by the doctor, we were able to talk, and they filled me in on a few more details.

"You were playing the Erie Otters," my mom said, reaching for my hand from her seat next to my bed. "You were getting the puck from behind your net when you got hit."

"But I was wearing a helmet," I replied. "How did my head get so messed up?"

From the other side of the room, my dad cleared his throat. My dad is as tough as they come. He was a firefighter for twenty-five years, and he can't bear to see my brother or me hurt in any way. He usually asks my mom to handle it. When I'd broken my wrist two years earlier, he dropped me off at the hospital with my mom and waited for us in the parking lot. But he was there now, which told me how serious my situation really was.

"When you were hit, your helmet popped off," he said. "Your head hit the metal stanchion that holds the glass."

"You were just lying there on the ice." My mom squeezed my hand tighter. I later learned that she had fainted in the stands. "I've never been so scared in my life."

"You don't remember any of this?" Chris asked.

"No, nothing." It was weird seeing my brother so concerned about me.

"Are you sure you're feeling okay?"

"Yeah, I feel fine. I'm just nervous about all these tests."

The doctors were a bit mystified as to why I wasn't experiencing any postconcussion symptoms, and they were running some key tests to find out what was going on. They warned me that I might need brain surgery. It wouldn't be pretty. The high-risk procedure would involve them removing a piece of my skull to clean up the bleeding. The rest of my life I would have a soft spot on my head, which meant that any intense physical activity would be out of the question. I found this all very difficult to process. I wanted the doctors to do everything they could to help me, but the very thought of having my brain operated on freaked me out.

On the seventh day of my hospital stay, my doctor ordered one more MRI to see if the bleeding in my brain had cleared up. If it had, I could go home. If not, I was going into surgery right away. They wanted to move quickly, so while we waited for the results of the MRI, the nurses started to glue beads onto my head.

"This is a standard preoperation routine," one of the nurses said. "We're mapping out where the doctors will operate."

My mom was next to me, praying—we were both scared about the risks involved in brain surgery. As the nurses continued to prep me, my dad entered into the room.

"Ben, I'm going to go start the van and pull it up front," he said in a chipper voice. "That way, when we get the good news that you don't need surgery, you can just come downstairs and the van will be warm and we can head home."

"We haven't heard from the doctor yet, Dad."

"I know. But I'll be ready when we do."

My dad's confidence reassured me, and sure enough, two hours later, the doctor told me that the results of the MRI were good.

"We're not able to explain it, Ben, but you don't seem to have any lingering issues. You can head home today."

"Thank you," I said, choking up. I felt like I had dodged a bullet.

Just as my dad had predicted, I was going home. When they wheeled me downstairs and out the sliding doors, my dad was waiting with the van nice and warm. I'll never forget that drive. All I could think was that I could have been out cold on an operating table at that very moment, but instead I was sitting in the back of the van headed home. While I had a long road to recovery in front of me, it didn't seem so scary anymore. *Maybe I will play hockey again*, I thought.

A few days after I was back in Oakville, Gabriel Landeskog and Ryan Murphy, two of my teammates, came over to see me.

"Ben, we've been so worried about you. How are you?" Gabe said.

"I'm actually doing pretty well. Just taking everything slowly."

"We wanted to visit you in the hospital," Murph said. "But the doctors told us that you needed to rest."

"I appreciate you guys stopping by. I won't be back on the ice for a while, so it's good to see you."

"If there's anything you need, Ben, just let us know. We're here for you," Gabe said.

"I will."

Because of the severity of my injury, I wasn't allowed to do much. I wanted to get better as fast as I could, but I knew the only way for me to heal properly was to take it slow. I remembered how when our team was losing, Steve would always say, "Find a way." Find a way to get a goal, stop a play, any little thing to turn the tide. I took that advice to heart.

While my body wasn't sore, I did suffer from fatigue, drowsiness, memory loss, and headaches. The doctors told me that the brain heals the most during sleep, so I slept a lot, especially during those first few weeks back. My mom would often check on me while I was sleeping, which I didn't realize right away.

"I felt like someone was pushing me awake last night," I said one morning. "Maybe it was a dream, though."

My mom started to laugh. "That was me!" she said. "You were sleeping so deeply I pushed you awake. You opened your eyes then immediately fell back to sleep."

At first, the only physical activity the doctors allowed me to do was walk around the block twice, once a day. I wanted to go further, but if I tried to push it, I would start to feel extremely tired, even though I wasn't walking that fast. It was only when I felt like I could walk the route at 110 percent that I let myself go a little farther, a little faster.

After my daily walk, I would come home and do Sudoku puzzles and word searches, also recommended by the doctors, to strengthen my brain.

I did some research about what foods help the brain recover faster from concussions and then I changed my diet, adding more fish and omega-3s. If something was good for my cognitive enhancement, I tried it. I was determined to do everything I could to get back on the ice.

Two months after my injury, I felt more like myself. I graduated from walking to light jogging, and then I started going to the gym. I was still getting my strength back, so I wasn't able to push myself as hard as I used to. I had all this energy, but nowhere to release it. Often I would just pace around the house.

Finally my mom said, "Ben, you're starting to drive me crazy."

"Sorry, Mom. I just don't know what to do with myself."

"Have you thought about going back to Kitchener and being with the team? Not playing, of course," she quickly added. "But maybe you should try to do a couple classes?"

I wasn't supposed to go back to school for two years, so the fact that my mom was suggesting that I try was a good sign that I was getting better. We spoke with the doctors, who were also impressed with my progress, and while they vetoed my playing hockey, they agreed that getting back into my old routine was the right next step.

But would the team have me? I went to Spotter to find out. "I'm ready to come back to the team. The doctors said it was okay."

"That's great news, Ben!" he said. "I want you to know that this door is always open to you. We've kept your locker stall in the dressing room. For the next five years, you're a part of this team, as much as you want to be."

I was overwhelmed with gratitude. All I could say was thank you.

I went back to live with the Brums, who were incredibly supportive, and when I showed up at the rink, everyone from the coaching staff and the trainers to my teammates welcomed me back with open arms.

Gabe came up to me right away. "We're so glad to have you back!" he said, patting me on the back.

Our captain, Dan Kelly, looked me up and down. "Did you leave your upper body in your other shirt?" he asked, referring to the weight I'd lost.

"I must have," I replied, laughing. It felt good that he was teasing me just like he would any other rookie on the team.

Sitting around with him, Gabe, Murph, Ben, and all the other guys on the team was the best recovery I could have asked for. *It's almost like I never left*, I thought.

I wasn't allowed to practice or play with the team, but I had started skating again casually on my own time, always wearing a doctor-prescribed helmet. I missed being with the guys, though.

*A year after my injury, I was allowed back
on the ice, but only when I was wearing my
silver cage, a helmet no one else had to wear.*

One day when everyone thought I was at the gym working out, I decided to sneak onto the ice during a practice. I don't know who I was fooling. I was the only player out there skating a mile a minute with a big silver cage of a helmet on his head and a huge smile on his face.

"Fanelli!" Spotter yelled. "Get off the ice this second!"

Damn.

Indefinitely benched, I did everything else I could to support the guys. I tracked stats, charted face-offs, went on road trips and to team events. I even filled the water bottles in the dressing room.

I can't put into words how incredible it felt to have that schedule and camaraderie again. There were still tough days. Watching the guys play in an arena packed with fans and not being out there with them made me feel sick to my stomach. But whenever I was upset, the boys and the training staff cheered me up and helped me stay hopeful that I would one day return to the ice if I just kept grinding away.

In February, when I went to speak to my neurologist about my progress, I expected to hear good news.

"I'm happy with how far you've come, Ben," he began. "But I can't clear you to play hockey." He went on to reiterate what the doctor had told me when I woke up in the hospital. "I think it's time to prepare yourself that you won't be able to play competitive sports ever again."

Before he was even done speaking, I got up out of my chair and ran down the hall, dropping to my knees in front of the elevator. I wanted nothing more than to be back out there with Gabe and Murph and the team and play for our fans. I started to realize that wasn't going to happen.

I went back to Kitchener, to the sidelines, but I couldn't bring myself to tell any of my teammates what had happened. All I could think to do was continue to train so that, if someone did give me a chance, I would be ready. When I wasn't training, I was catching up in school so that I could graduate on time. It was the only way forward I knew.

A year after my injury, I went into the hospital for a grueling three-and-a-half-hour cognitive exam, which I passed with flying colours. In fact, I performed better than I had before I was injured, and when the doctor showed me my latest brain scan, all the injured areas were completely healed. I was overjoyed, and my anger about being held back from playing hockey dissipated. Clearly, my brain had needed that time to recover. Everything in my life, mentally and physically, was on track once more. The neurologist hadn't cleared me for sports, but I was allowed to start training harder, which meant I could do a drill or two in practice that had zero chance of contact.

I sat down with my parents, Rob, and Spotter to discuss my role on the team.

"There's no need to rush your progress," my mom started.

"We're not going anywhere," Spotter said. "I know you're in top shape, but let's make sure there are no other issues."

Rob agreed. "We're so impressed with your recovery, Ben, but we want to be absolutely certain that you're ready to play."

Before, I might have pushed back, but seeing that brain scan made me realize what one year could do. When I returned to the game, I wanted to be able to give everything I had, which included a fully recovered brain, and so we decided I would sit out one more year.

That second year, I found that it was much more difficult not to be on the ice. I wasn't deep in recovery mode anymore and I had graduated high school—on time—and needed a distraction, something to pour all my bottled-up energy into.

I itched to get back, to put on that jersey. I missed lining up before a game, hearing my name being called over the loudspeaker, taking the first strides on fresh ice with a stick in my hand. I started sneaking into practice again and hoped no one would notice I was playing. I tried to gauge the mood of the coaches and check out which drills the team was doing to see if it was a good day for me to try and get into practice unnoticed. If we were doing a really safe drill with no chance of contact, Spotter let me participate, but other days, he had no patience for my tricks.

He'd catch me in a lineup for an exercise. "Fanelli, is that you? Get off the ice now!"

I hung my head like a puppy in trouble and skated off. "Sorry, Spotter."

I was determined to show everyone, especially my mom, that I was ready to do something more intense, so I decided to put all my excess energy towards training for a triathlon. I was too big to be competitive, but I wanted the challenge, and when the guys were on the ice, I was in the gym, cycling, swimming, and running. The day of the competition, I saw some Kitchener Rangers fans in the crowd. *Wow, I can't believe they came out to cheer me on,* I thought. *This is my chance to prove my strength.* My parents were there waiting for me as I crossed the finish line.

"You did it, Ben!" my dad said.

"You've come so far since your injury," my mom added. "We're proud of you."

"Remember when you could only walk around the block?" My dad chuckled. "Look at you now!"

I was out of breath, but I had a huge smile on my face. I had done it. There wasn't anything that could stop me now. After that, I was cleared by my doctors to return to the game.

In the dressing room before my first full-contact practice, I felt a mix of confidence and nerves as I laced up my skates. I was ready to get back to work, but then again, it had been so long since I'd really practiced with the team. What if I was rusty?

When I hit the ice, the guys all gave a cheer. "He's back!" someone said. Then I heard Spotter's voice. "I guess you don't have to sneak into practice today, Fanelli."

I did a few laps around the ice, and as I was crossing the spot where I got injured, Gabe charged into me.

"What was that f—" I started to say, then I saw his smile.

"I wanted to hit you right away so you wouldn't be nervous. Now you know you're going to be fine." He chuckled, then skated away.

Turns out, that was exactly what I needed. The rest of the practice went off without a hitch.

———

"You haven't lost your stride, Fanelli," Spotter said as I came off the ice. "You're going to make it back and play a real game. You stay healthy and give every practice 110 percent of your focus and you'll be successful."

He might have a fiery temper, but Spotter was always in tune with how his players were feeling.

And just like that, I slipped into a comfortable groove. I was officially a hockey player again.

My first regular-season game was something I looked forward to for weeks. The game was against the Windsor Spitfires, and we were playing on home ice. When they announced my name in the opening ceremonies, they projected my photo onto the rink, and I skated out to the centre. I was in awe as all those in the arena rose to their feet. *Everyone in here is cheering for me*, I thought. *I hope I make them proud.*

The whole game was surreal, like time was standing still. There was a time when I hadn't thought that day would ever happen, and yet, there I was. I was focused on one thing: playing the best hockey I could. Because I had no memory or flashbacks of that terrible hit, whenever I went behind the net or into the corner to get the puck, I had no fear. Getting hit didn't bother me either—I had Gabe to thank for that. We won 4–3. I was back.

Halfway through the season, Steve came to me with some news.

"Ben, did you hear? Julian is being traded to Oshawa."

Julian Melchiori was a good friend of mine. "Oh, wow, he must be so excited."

"We're going to need you on the ice more. How do you feel about taking on extra responsibility?"

"I would love that," I said without hesitation. "Thanks, Steve." *I guess I'm not just playing again*, I thought. *I'm playing well.*

After the trade, I took on a bigger role with the team, which led to my being named the alternate captain the next year, and the captain the year after that. I was wearing the *C* on my jersey, just like Derek Roy and Mike Richards had worn it before me. I was so humbled to have the honour of leading the Rangers in my final year, and when the season ended, I never had to wonder "What if?" I'd done it. I'd made a comeback and played 194 games after suffering a severe head injury that could have ended things for me. I had determined that I would not be limited by my body.

I wouldn't have been able to make my comeback without the support of my team and my community. Lance Armstrong has always been a hero of mine, and when I found out that his Livestrong Foundation was hosting a charity bike ride with Lance in Kitchener, I immediately went to Michelle Fortin at the Rangers office.

"I know this is a long shot," I said. "But is there any chance I could run up to Lance when he's in town and say hi? I just want to shake his hand and get a photo with him."

My last game as captain of the Kitchener Rangers, we took a moment at centre ice to salute our fans for supporting us all year. After, I did a lap around the rink and received an incredible standing ovation from the best fans in hockey.

"I don't know, Ben," Michelle answered. "But let me see what I can do."

She connected me with the event organizers, who told me that anyone could bike with Lance for sixty seconds of the ride, but he or she had to raise at least $10,000 for the Grand River Regional Cancer Centre. There was no way I had that kind of money. I wasn't even sure if I could raise it in time. But this is how incredible my community is: two anonymous individuals donated the money so that I could take part in the ride.

At the time of event, I weighed 215 pounds, which is good for hockey, but not for cycling. Everyone flew by me, but I did get that one minute with Lance at the beginning of the race. I couldn't believe I was actually riding next to him, but I collected myself enough to tell him that how he overcame cancer inspired me during my own recovery. He thanked me for sharing my story and we chatted about hockey until it was someone else's turn to ride with him. I'll never forget that day.

When I started playing hockey again, I decided that I wanted to give back somehow to other brain injury survivors and also spread the word about the dangers of concussions and brain injuries. My family thought it was a great idea. Since my injury, I'd grown much closer to my brother Chris.

"Maybe your story can inspire someone else struggling with a brain injury," he said.

"And show them it's better to take the time to heal," my mom added.

With the help of Michelle and Rob, I founded Head Strong: Fanelli for Brain Injury Awareness, which eventually grew into the EMPWR Foundation, a charitable organization that supports better recovery for concussion injuries and provides a platform for athletes to share their personal experiences with injury. Through EMPWR,

I've had the opportunity to run workshops with teams, schools, community groups, and businesses. The biggest thing I've learned is that the support I received from my team and my community is almost unheard of. We have incredible scientists making strides in research, but many athletes who have to take time away from their sport don't have such a strong support system.

I never made it to the NHL, but hockey has remained a central part of my life. I'm currently the assistant coach with the University of Waterloo hockey program, and because of my experience, I'm better able to help players when they're injured. If I see a player get rocked with a hard hit, I make sure to check with the trainers before he gets back in the game. Often a player will push hard to return to the ice because, from the time he started playing hockey, he's been told that if he doesn't play through injury, he's soft. He's been taught that it's the responsibility of each player to do everything he can to bring the team to victory, no matter what sacrifice that demands. That pressure is why so many injured athletes return to the game too soon. In my role, I make a point to talk to players who might be masking pain and reassure them that in the long run, it's better for them and their team to sit out a couple of games than to have their career cut short by injury.

We're at a point now where everyone and their brother knows someone who has been through a concussion and has witnessed firsthand the impact that injury has on them, their family, and their friends. That means things are starting to move in the right direction. Hockey will always have risks—it's a high-speed game with contact—but players are thinking twice before taking a run at an opponent in a vulnerable position.

And when injuries do happen, the dialogue is different. When New York Ranger Jimmy Vesey announced on Twitter that he had a concussion, his captain, Rick Nash, responded by saying that Jimmy should take some time off. As a young player fighting to prove himself in the NHL, Jimmy was probably reluctant to take the necessary time to recover from his injury, but Rick was setting a good example by encouraging him to take care of himself. To top it off, another one of my heroes, Marc Savard—who was forced to retire because of concussions and head injuries—retweeted the exchange and said, "If you want someone to talk to, send me a message." This has nothing to do with research, rehab, or physio, but it has everything to do with the support of the team and hockey community, and that's what hockey is all about. In dressing rooms and arenas across the country, there's a camaraderie, respect, and generosity that you can't find anywhere else.

When people ask me about that night I got hit, I always say that those three seconds changed my life for the better. My injury made me a stronger person and gave me a greater sense of purpose—it helped me find my way.

Ben Fanelli is a former OHL defenceman and captain of the Kitchener Rangers. In 2012, he was named the OHL's Humanitarian of the Year. Ben is a coach, a speaker, and the founder of Head Strong (now EMPWR) and HeroicMinds, a podcast and website dedicated to equipping those facing adversity with the tools they need to overcome hardship. Follow him on Twitter at @Ben_Fanelli_.

Saving the Game I Love

Dr. Charles Tator

Hockey is too good a game not to try to save.

This can happen in a hockey game? It was the first thought I had as I examined my first hockey player with a broken neck. He was a junior hockey player, known for his strong defence, who had broken his neck during a game. He had been hit from behind and had gone headfirst into the boards. Given the severity of his injury, I wasn't confident that he would be returning to the ice.

This was the seventies, and I was a recent graduate of the University of Toronto's training program in neurosurgery. Even my senior colleagues were also surprised that we were seeing far more spinal cord injuries in hockey players than in the old days. Although some of these players recovered very well, even to resume playing hockey, there was a worrying number of players who would be confined to a wheelchair for the rest of their lives. Even more troubling was that many of these players were teenagers. The question on all our minds was: *What can we do about these injuries?*

I knew hockey could be quite rough. The sport has been a passion of mine since childhood. I grew up in the Forest Hill neighborhood of Toronto in the thirties and forties, and Lou Turofsky, the Toronto Maple Leafs team photographer, lived right next door. I acted as his "bulb boy" for the home games at Maple Leaf Gardens. In those days, photographers had to carry around extra bulbs because the cameras got only one picture per bulb. I would follow Mr. Turofsky around at rink-side carrying a satchel filled with fresh flashbulbs. In between shots, I'd watch my heroes skate by. After the game, we would go into the dressing room, where Lou would take more photos. I met all the greats—Syl Apps, Turk Broda, Teeder Kennedy, Howie Meeker—and often had my picture taken with many of them, too. Talk about a perk of the job!

Toronto was a lot different back then. When I wasn't working as a bulb boy at Maple Leaf Gardens, I was listening to games on the radio or skating to school. That's right, skating. West Prep School was only a couple of blocks from my house, and we got so much snow and ice in those days that I could skate across lawns, driveways, and roads and be at school in record time. We had a great "cushion," or hockey rink, at the school maintained by Mr. Fitzell, the caretaker.

Despite my passion for the game, I was an exceptionally mediocre hockey player. However, I was good enough to make my high school team, but I never had any aspirations of playing in the NHL. Of course, that didn't stop me from finding other ways to emulate the players I looked up to.

"Make me look like Howie Meeker," I said to our local barber one day. Back then, Howie had a brush cut and I thought it was neat.

My mother was not impressed. "You barely have any hair left!"

She was right, but at least I looked like Howie, my idol.

When I was eighteen, I was still hockey crazy, but I had begun to think about what I might do for a career. I decided to become a doctor, mainly because I watched so many in my family suffer from various illnesses growing up. Doctors weren't the most revered people in my family, because of some medical mishaps. I'd always been interested in the brain and loved the idea of being able to help people with brain problems. Psychiatry was my initial interest, but when I

Here I am at seventeen with my high school senior hockey team,
the Forest Hill Falcons. I'm in the front row, third from the left.

saw people desperately ill because of brain tumours and blood clots
in the brain walk out of the hospital after neurosurgery, I said, "I
want to do that!"

When I began treating hockey players with broken necks, I was
confronted with the necessity of combining my neurosurgical training with my love of hockey. What could I do about these young players who were suffering life-changing injuries in the game I loved?

I looked to my mentor, Dr. Tom Pashby, an ophthalmologist who
was tirelessly advocating for the use of helmets and face guards in
hockey. As the consulting doctor for the Leafs, he had seen a number
of blind eyes from hockey and other sports, and he used his position
as chair of the Canadian Standards Association to fight for the mandatory use of helmets in the NHL, a rule that came into effect in 1979,
just a few years after he began campaigning for better equipment.

"It's always better to prevent an injury than to try and repair it after the fact," he would always say. "We just have to persevere and we'll get their attention."

I went back to my hockey-player patients' charts and studied their X-rays, then I watched videos of the hits that caused their injuries. We even had some NHL footage. We started a search across the country for similar cases, and my colleagues in other cities sent me their records. We figured it out! Almost half of these broken necks and spinal cord injuries were caused by hits from behind that propelled the unsuspecting players into the boards. In many cases, the players were almost horizontal when they hit the boards, which caused a vertebra in the neck to explode because of the extreme compressive force. This is what we call a burst fracture—the bone bursts and crushes the adjacent spinal cord, causing major damage. In other cases, the unsuspected impact would force the player's head forwards and downwards, almost touching his chest, causing dislocation of the bones and crushing the spinal cord. Both types were frightening injuries that left many players in a wheelchair for life.

We also found that many young athletes were busy strengthening their arms and legs but did nothing to strengthen their neck muscles. By the nineties, we had dozens of cases of broken necks in hockey reported to us, and the most startling fact was that when we searched the old records, we found only rare cases before 1970. Thus, this was a relatively new phenomenon we were dealing with, and it was caused by the emergence of a more aggressive, violent style of play.

We wrote papers in medical journals and gave lectures on our findings, but we knew we needed Hockey Canada on our side if we were to get real change. The organization put me in touch with Todd Jackson, its director of insurance and risk management.

I filled him in on our findings. "It all comes down to the way guys are hitting each other, Todd. Hitting an unsuspecting player from behind never used to be part of the game, but we're seeing more and

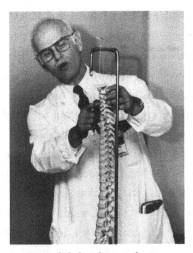

*A candid shot from a demon-
stration on how the spinal cord is
damaged when a player is hit from
behind and crashes into the boards.*

more reckless play, and 'win at all costs.'" While there were rules regarding hitting from behind in the Hockey Canada and NHL rule books, they were not being enforced.

Todd nodded.

"For the safety of the players, we'd recommend you implement a specific penalty for this kind of hit."

"We're very committed to injury prevention," Todd replied. "Other than a new penalty, what else can we do?"

"We can develop an injury prevention committee, and figure out the best ways to educate players about the dangers of hitting from behind."

"I like the sound of that," Todd said.

He was great to work with and agreed to join the committee. Jack Cooper, the owner of Cooper Canada, was also on board.

"I want to get violence out of the game," he said more than once. "I want kids to be safe so that they can play the game forever."

I couldn't agree more. With the support of Jack, as well as Murray Costello, the head of Hockey Canada, and with the support of the National Hockey League Players' Association, Canadian Tire, CCM, and Bauer, we created a program at ThinkFirst Canada to educate all amateur hockey players about safety. A man by the name of Kevin Stubbington from Windsor invented the Stop sign badge that was sewn onto the back of hockey sweaters to remind players not to hit from behind, and Hockey Canada and Campbell Soup distributed them. At ThinkFirst Canada (now Parachute Canada), we created a number of great safety videos with the help of hockey guru Al Stewart. Al, whose résumé included working for Conn Smythe and Harold Ballard, founded the production company that established *Coach's Corner*, and he graciously donated his resources to our cause.

Our ThinkFirst Smart Hockey videos starred hockey greats like Mike Bossy and Mats Sundin, who taught young hockey hopefuls how to play the game smarter and safer. The area three to four feet away from the boards was identified as the most dangerous on the ice—that's where players are most likely to be surprised with a hit from behind, and then strike the boards. But the game requires that players often move through that space, so Mike and Mats demonstrated how players should go into the boards on a small angle to get the puck and protect themselves at the same time. "Never go at a right angle into the boards," they said. We sold about forty thousand videos for five dollars each at Canadian Tire, and a dollar of every sale went toward our injury-prevention program at ThinkFirst Canada. Through our combined initiatives, awareness seemed to be growing, and in emergency departments across Canada, doctors began to see a decline in the number of serious neck injuries.

In the 1996–1997 season, the NHL introduced a separate penalty for charging a player from behind that carried more weight. While I was thrilled to see we were making a difference, violence in hockey didn't seem to be dropping. Even after tougher penalties were implemented, there was a noticeable shift in playing attitude, a new hit-him-hard mind-set that seemed to focus not on knocking the opponent off the puck, but knocking him out cold. Players were revered for their ability to knock opponents unconscious! Head hits were encouraged in some hockey circles, and the number of concussions increased enormously.

It saddened me to see a game I loved so much become so unsafe because of head hits. But when I saw the same behaviour infiltrate the minor and junior hockey leagues, I became worried. At one of my son's hockey games, I heard a coach telling my son's team that the only way to stop the star player on the opposing team was to "kill him, and take him out of the game." Of course, the coach didn't want the star player dead, but he was so worked up that he was using violent rhetoric to get his players to do whatever they could to win. A fistfight followed between the coach and the father of the opposing team's star. It wasn't long after that that my son hung up his skates.

Every time I saw players swinging sticks, hitting from behind, and brawling on TV, I winced because I knew what was happening to their brains—I saw the fallout of on-ice fights in my patients: concussions. The thing about concussions is that they're hard to detect unless you know what you're looking for. They don't show up on X-rays or in brain scans, and sometimes the symptoms don't appear until hours or days after the injury, so it's easy for a concussion to go undiagnosed. And what I was quickly learning was that a concussed brain is highly vulnerable to further damage.

I started seeing patients as young as twelve years old suffering from concussions they'd received on the ice. Teenagers are more susceptible to concussions because they are skating faster than they ever have before and they weigh more than they did when they were ten or eleven, but they don't yet know how to throw their weight around safely. We learned that teenagers also need more time to recover from concussions than adults do because their brains are growing at exponential rates. But they were not taking sufficient time away from the game to allow their brains to recover. Many of my patients were already showing signs of brain damage at the ages of twelve and thirteen—they had difficulty remembering what they had for breakfast, and they were falling behind in school. *Some of these kids should never play hockey again*, I thought.

I couldn't help but conjure up my memories of those early winter mornings when I was so excited to lace up my skates and skate to my elementary school, or the joyous hours of playing hockey on my high school and faculty of medicine hockey teams. I became a doctor to help people. I had to add concussions to my bucket list of preventable catastrophic injuries in hockey. I started thinking about ways to eliminate concussions in all levels of hockey.

We gave lectures to coaches in the Greater Toronto Hockey League, spoke at annual Hockey Canada meetings, and wrote about the damage of sports concussions in medical journals. Murray and Todd were instrumental in getting us in front of the right people, as was René Fasel at the International Ice Hockey Federation.

"The first step is prevention," I would tell people. "We know we can't eliminate contact on the ice, so let's find ways to cut down on the frequency of collisions and the impact of them."

We advocated for the NHL to enlarge the ice surface to match the international size, which would open up the game and limit the number of collisions. The international rink size was only fifteen feet wider, but the NHL have yet to change the size of the rinks. A likely explanation is that they would lose revenue if the first few rows of seats were converted to ice. There was also concern that fans would be disappointed if there wasn't as much contact.

"They'll lose a couple of bucks, but they'll save a lot of lives," I said to anyone who would listen. *Persevere and get their attention*, I reminded myself over and over again.

I had often talked to Tom Pashby and Jack Cooper about the equipment. "Do the shoulder and elbow pads need to be as hard as steel? When I played, they were designed to protect the player wearing them, but we're seeing players use them as offensive weapons." Certain NHL stars were actually revered in some circles for their ability to knock out opponents with their shoulder pads!

"I'm with you," they said. "The regulations need to change."

The NHL did end up softening the pads, but insufficiently so, because elbows and shoulders are still delivering blows that cause too many concussions. I feel we still have a lot farther to go, especially when it comes to treating concussed players. When prevention fails—and we know it sometimes will—the best thing we can do is diagnose concussed players immediately and remove them from the game. Then we can work with them to reintroduce their physical activity gradually and in a safe space, because if a player sustains a second injury without having had the chance to recover from the first, he can aggravate his symptoms, making them last longer, and even risking death.

NHL teams have their own doctors to diagnosis concussions and treat affected players, but amateur players don't, so we implemented a program called the Concussion Roadshow and went across the country for several years training minor- and junior-league coaches to recognize when one of their players had a concussion. For the most part, the program was accepted, but some parents didn't want to take their concussed kids out of the game, and some coaches didn't want to tone down the rougher style of play. Furthermore, we still had the problem of the pros. The kids are still watching too aggressive, too violent professional hockey.

It was frustrating to see that resistance, especially knowing what happens when concussed players aren't given the treatment they need. I remember having to tell a star player that he couldn't play hockey anymore. He was just a teenager and he had to retire. It was one of the most difficult conversations I've ever had because it meant that we did not have a treatment to restore brain function that was lost. For him, prevention was too late, and treatment had not yet been discovered to reverse the damage. Quitting hockey was essential for him to maintain the brain function that remained and to give nature a chance to restore at least some of the brain function that had been lost due to the game that he and I loved.

"I'm sorry it's not good news," I said to him. "You've had three concussions now and you're already experiencing severe memory problems."

"Are you sure, Dr. Tator?" he asked.

I could see the heartbreak in his eyes, and I felt it, too. We both hated the thought that he would never play again.

"Your brain simply can't take another concussion. For your own health, you have to quit."

In the last ten years, I've been in this situation a hundred times, and I've had to recommend young people stop playing collision sports like hockey because their brain could not tolerate any more battering. I knew what would happen if they didn't.

Don Sanderson was a senior hockey player known for his scrappy style. In December 2008, he got into a fight during a game and his helmet came off, and when he fell to the ice, he hit his head hard. He slipped into a coma and died three weeks later. He was just twenty-one years old. I don't know if he had a history of concussions, but this accident shows just how fragile the brain is and how devastating violence on the ice can be.

It's times like these I think of Jack Cooper's mantra about ensuring kids can play hockey forever, and I remind myself that we can't give up, that we will find a way to make hockey safer for everyone.

The pros have been tough to bring to the table. So, with a colleague, the neurologist Dr. Richard Wennberg, we extended a study on sports-induced brain injuries started by a *Toronto Star* sports reporter, the late Randy Starkman. We did copious research on all the players who had to quit hockey because of concussions and for whom in many in cases the owners had to continue paying their large, multimillion-dollar salaries for the remaining number of years

In my role at ThinkFirst, I go to schools to teach kids about the importance of injury prevention. Here I am with some elementary school students.

of their contracts. From 1995 to 2015, we calculated the financial impact on the league of NHL players forced to retire because of concussions. We identified thirty-five players—guys like Eric Lindros and Marc Savard—and discovered the total cost to teams and insurers for career-ending concussions was USD $135,476,777. We published our findings in 2016, and while we've had no direct response from the NHL as of this writing, we are seeing fewer enforcers in the NHL, so perhaps the message that violent play is expensive may be starting to have an effect.

Thanks to extensive research, we are starting to understand the long-term effects of concussions. We know now that repeated concussions in some hockey players can lead to an untreatable neurodegenerative disease known as chronic traumatic encephalopathy (CTE). The most common symptoms include dementia, aggression, depression, and suicidal behaviour, and currently the only way to diagnose CTE is through an autopsy.

It took us decades to get to this conclusion. For some time, CTE was thought to affect only boxers, which is why it was so commonly referred to as punch-drunk syndrome, a spin on the Latin *dementia pugilistica*. And then, in the early 2000s, the first professional football players were diagnosed with CTE. Still, it wasn't until 2009 that the first hockey player was tested for CTE. Reg Fleming was a twelve-year NHL defenceman, and his brain showed that he did indeed suffer from CTE. Since then we've seen a few more cases, but no one really knows how many hockey players have suffered from CTE and gone undiagnosed.

In 2010, we started the Canadian Concussion Centre at Toronto Western Hospital to try to find some better ways to detect early signs that concussions are taking a toll on the brain and to see if we could discover some treatments for concussion-induced brain damage. In 2015, Steve Montador, a former Chicago Blackhawks defenceman, died unexpectedly in his home. I knew Steve through his father Paul, who was on our board of directors for ThinkFirst and Parachute Canada. A few years before Steve's death, Paul and I were both in Vancouver, and Paul invited me to come watch Steve play against the Vancouver Canucks. I jumped at the chance and ended up witnessing Steve score one of his thirty-three career NHL goals.

After the game, Paul and I waited outside the dressing room for Steve to appear. I met him and we chatted about hockey and the latest advancements in treating sports-related brain injuries. Steve was open about the concussions he'd suffered and some of the issues he faced as a result. For example, he showed me his sunken, fractured cheekbone from a blow to the face that had not healed perfectly and was producing some discomfort. His father told him that one of my projects involved examining the brains of concussed players after their death.

"The more research we do," I said to Steve, "the closer we will get to finding a solution to the long-term effects of concussions."

Steve was very interested in finding a way to prevent others from experiencing the same health issues he had. Steve looked at me thoughtfully and said, "Well, doc, you can have my brain."

"We don't want premature donations," I joked.

Steve died just five years later, at thirty-five. His father honoured Steve's commitment and ensured that his brain came to me for examination at the Canadian Concussion Centre. Based on Steve's medical records, I counted the number of concussions he had sustained—nineteen. We found deposits of an abnormal protein, p-tau, in several areas of his brain, an indication that he had CTE. This protein damages the brain and produces dementia and mental health disorders such as depression and impulsivity. His condition hadn't been as severe as others', but he was our youngest case. The knowledge was chilling—I had known him in life and here he was a victim of the condition I was trying to eradicate. His loss felt that much more personal. At present, CTE can be diagnosed only post-mortem, but medical research is getting closer to diagnosing CTE in living patients, and once that's possible, we might be able to find ways to treat the brain and prevent further damage so that people like Steve could have a long and happy life. I'd always dreamed of saving someone's life by removing a tumour from his brain, but I would be just as happy if I restored a life by removing p-tau.

As I said to Steve, the key to progress is in the research, and we hope that by raising awareness, everyone involved in hockey, from the leagues to the equipment suppliers, will see the need to fund our research initiative. It helps that pros like Ken Dryden, Eric Lindros, and Marc Savard are speaking out about how to eliminate needless head shots and make the sport safer without losing the important parts of the game. The closed shop of the past is over, and real change is on the horizon. In the last few years, I've found that I don't wince as much when I watch an NHL game, because the sport is evolving, and young, talented players like Connor McDavid and Auston Matthews are playing a skillful game, not a violent one.

I've loved hockey since the time I was a bulb boy at Maple Leaf Gardens, and I won't ever stop trying to make it safer. Hockey is too good a game not to try to save. And I know we can, if we work together.

Dr. Charles Tator is a Canadian neurosurgeon at Toronto Western Hospital and a professor of neurosurgery at the University of Toronto whose research has transformed our understanding of spinal cord injury and concussions. In 1992, he founded Think-First Canada, an injury-prevention foundation now merged into Parachute Canada, where he is a board member. He is an officer of the Order of Canada and has been inducted into the Canadian Medical Hall of Fame, the Terry Fox Hall of Fame, and Canada's Sports Hall of Fame. In 2012, he received USA Hockey's Excellence in Safety Award.

Fighting the Good Fight

Hilary Knight

Our fight was about equality, but we wouldn't have
been able to do it without creating a sense of unity
within the team and making sure that every player,
especially our rookies, felt like she was truly a part
of the team. That goal and that win was ours.

It was three days before the 2017 world championships, and we were still waiting to see if we would even compete. We wanted to play, of course—hockey was our lives and we were risking our careers by protesting USA Hockey for equitable support—but our fight was bigger than us: it was about the future of the game for girls and women. Our steps were to better represent the next generation coming up through the US national women's hockey program, and subsequently to inspire women in other industries to continue seeking equitable support and pushing for better standards. In doing so, we hoped to set greater precedent for women everywhere.

I had joined the US women's national team program in 2006. I was only seventeen, but I quickly learned that being a part of the team required an extraordinary amount of sacrifice and dedication. I was young and eager to win a gold medal, but I couldn't make ends meet on my hockey salary alone, and with my training and playing schedule, I didn't have time for a full-time job. I began giving lessons, teaching skating and hockey. I did everything: private lessons, group lessons, hockey camps. *At least I'm on the ice*, I would tell myself.

After ten years, I'd had enough, and so had the other women on our team. We were the right group of empowered women, and we were playing the best we ever had. Now was the time for change. If we didn't stand up for ourselves, who would?

In 2016, we quietly approached a law firm about our chances, and they began asking us questions about our working conditions. When they told us we were about twenty years behind the US women's soccer team, our conviction only grew stronger.

We were floored. We knew things were bad, but were we really two decades behind? It was like an onion: the more we peeled back the layers, the more we discovered, and the more we discovered, the more determined we were to establish new standards. We submitted our needs to USA Hockey, and then, on March 15, we announced that we were boycotting the world championships, which was just sixteen days away. It was a galvanizing moment for our team, our player pool, and any woman involved in hockey.

As the days passed, we fielded calls and advocated for equitable support, and we checked in with one another, because we knew our strength came from sticking together. But would that be enough? After almost two weeks had gone by, we had time for just one more practice before the world championships began, and we still hadn't heard an answer. *Hockey is worth this. Hockey will be better because of this*, I reminded myself. *After all, who would I be without the game?*

I fell in love with hockey when I was six years old after my dad's job relocated him from California to Illinois. If we had stayed on the West Coast, maybe I would have become a skier like the rest of my family, but there were no mountains in Illinois. There were rinks, though, and my mom made sure to sign up my younger brothers, James, Remington, and William, and me for hockey.

It was the speed that hooked me. Once I felt the rink air hit my face, I just wanted to learn how to go faster so that feeling would never leave. I started to notice that the older kids were whipping around the ice. *How are they so fast?* I wondered. I studied the way they were moving their feet, one in front of the other in quick succession—crossovers.

"I want to do that!" I told my mom.

I began practicing crossovers, slowly building my speed. I was obsessed. Once I tried a drill, I wanted to do it again right away. No one had ever told me what reps were, but I was doing them. I spent hours on the ice perfecting my edgework so that I was always balanced, especially when I bodychecked my brothers. As the oldest and only girl in our family, I was determined to show them how it was done and to be the best leader.

Here's a candid photo from my early hockey days. My mom is dutifully tying my skates while my grandmother watches on.

When it came to lifting the puck when I shot, I was a late bloomer. Most of the time that I managed to raise the puck, it was an accident, which stung, because my brothers were so good at shooting and could sink the puck into the net in different places confidently. I watched them shoot over and over again, then practiced until I could flick my wrist and send the puck flying into the net precisely where I wanted it to.

"I'm going to play for Team USA," I said to my grandmother. "I'm going to the Olympics."

She gave me a nice smile, then pulled my mom aside. "Cynthia, you know girls don't play hockey."

I heard that a lot. Aside from one year I spent on a girls' team, I played exclusively on boys' teams, and sometimes I was cut from the boys' teams because I was a girl. Meanwhile, my brothers were raking in state championships in hockey and almost every other sport they played.

That just spurred me on to be the best I could be.

"Hilary plays hockey, and if she says she's going to the Olympics, then she is," my mom replied.

I get my backbone from my mom. Her confidence in my ability to achieve my dreams helped me become the player and the person I am today.

"How did it go?" she would ask me when she picked me up from games and practices.

If I had a rough game and felt like I wasn't good enough, she would say, "Be the best competitor and the best person you can be, and things will fall into place. Don't worry. Just make sure you bust your butt and have fun."

And when people said I didn't belong, my mom was there to defend me. In her calm, cool way, she would silence those who said that the only reason I was on the hockey team was because I was a girl.

Even with my mom in my corner, it was tough being a girl in a male-dominated sport. Once I had to quit a team over halfway through the season because the environment was toxic. I hated the idea of quitting, but that experience taught me the importance of having the right people around me. As I waited for the next season, I played in summer tournaments.

I played every sport you could imagine—field hockey, lacrosse, soccer (I was big for a girl, so I made for a good goalie), baseball— but they all took a back seat to hockey. And nothing could stop me from playing the game. When I was twelve, I decided to go to Choate Rosemary Hall, a boarding school in Connecticut known for its excellent hockey program. Angela Ruggiero, a former Team USA hockey legend who I had seen win gold at the 1998 Winter Olympics in Nagano, had gone there, and I wanted to be just like her.

All my mom's friends were shocked that she was sending me to boarding school until she explained that it had been my idea. I wanted to be the next Joe Sakic, Pavel Bure, Brendan Shanahan, Cammi Granato. I would always sign my name in my school notes and write "soon to be famous" at the bottom.

My mom had fostered a sense of independence in me, and I was excited to embark on a new adventure and develop relationships on and off the ice. At Choate, I was never really homesick—that's how much I enjoyed being on my own and focusing on honing my skills. Every day when I passed by Angela Ruggiero's picture, I told myself that I would do what she did.

The school's hockey program put me on the national team's radar. In 2006, the summer between my junior and senior year of high school, I received a letter inviting me to go to Team USA's under-twenty-two (U-22) selection camp that fall. *This is my chance to make the team*, I thought excitedly.

There was nothing I wanted more than to represent my country on the international stage. I had gone to the open tryouts for the 2006 Olympic team the year before, but I had been cut. Hockey can be humbling in that way. The rejection was hard to swallow, but my next thought was, *What do I need to do to get back here as a stronger player?*

Going into camp, I determined to be a sponge and learn as much as I could from everyone on the team. I was incredibly happy to be chosen for the U-22 team, but I saw it as a step in the right direction. I wasn't content just being in the program—I needed to grow and develop as a player, especially if I was going to make it to the next Olympics.

Later that year, I attended my first senior training camp, the memory of which will forever be burned in my mind. In the van ride to the rink, I pulled out my binder to go over my homework. I was still in school and needed to maximize the hours I had in the day so that I could focus on hockey. On the front of my binder, I had taped a cool fisheye photo in the front sleeve of Krissy Wendell, the team's forward, who was setting records in the NCAA. The next thing I knew, Krissy was sitting right next to me in the van. I instantly closed my binder and shoved it back into my bag. She never said anything, which I was grateful for—it was embarrassing—but to this day, I still wonder if she noticed.

One thing the camp showed me was exactly what it took to play at the Olympic level. I just had to get there. In the meantime, I was part of the national team, competing in the 4 Nations tournament and the world championships, and being mentored by my older teammates, not just in hockey, but in school as well. Some would act as my quiz proctors, others as my flash card study buddies. One of my teammates was a pro at SAT prep and would quiz me whenever I passed her getting on or off the bus. Even though I wasn't going to the Olympics, I knew I had found an amazing group of women, all of whom were true leaders, to play hockey with.

My next step was to find the right university to develop my skills as a player. And that was the exciting part. During the fall of my senior year of high school, I received letters every day from schools all over the country offering me a scholarship to play on their team. Some of these coaches were idols of mine, and they wanted *me* on their team— I felt like a kid in a candy shop each time I checked the mail.

While I was flattered by all the offers, I really had my eye on one school and one team only. I wanted to be a Badger at the University of Wisconsin. It had been a dream of mine to go to Dartmouth, but as soon as I visited Wisconsin, I knew I couldn't go anywhere else. The school had a dynamite athletic program and was coming off a national championship win. When they offered me a scholarship, there was no doubt in my mind that I would accept.

At Wisconsin, we had the best of everything, the white-glove treatment, as they say, and as a result, we played our best. Our team was stacked with talent, and we all pushed each other to be better. It was the perfect recipe for developing my skills, and it showed. In 2008, during my first year there, the national team called me back to compete at the world championships in China, and we won gold. Just the year before, I'd been left off the roster, and now I was part of a gold-medal team.

That's when I really broke out as a hockey player. In my second season with the Badgers, the whole team was on fire. Surrounded by great players, I was able to put up some personal-best numbers. During the national championships, we didn't just beat our competition, we pounded them and went on to win it all. Those were the golden years for the Badgers.

In 2009, the national team named me to the roster of players going to the 2010 Olympics in Vancouver. It was a dream come true, one of the most magical moments in my life. Finally, after fifteen years of dreaming, I was going to get a chance to wear the US flag on my jersey at the Olympics. I took a year off from the Badgers to train, and the team was in top shape going into the games. There, we won every game leading up to the finals against Canada. They'd taken gold the last two years, and we wanted desperately to upset them, but we were playing on their home ice and the crowd was definitely a factor. We ended up losing 2–0.

My mom was incredibly proud of me, but torn up at how badly I had wanted to win gold. At the Olympics, team sports have tunnel vision. On one end, all we see is gold, that's the reason we're competing, but on the other end, we see the bigger picture—being an Olympian and being able to change the world through sport. So while not taking home gold was disappointing, I was happy that I had achieved my goal of making it to the Olympics, and I vowed that next time, we'd be wearing gold around our necks.

By 2012, I had my history degree, lifelong friends, and a thousand great memories on and off the ice, and my place with the US national team was secure. I entered the Canadian Women's Hockey League draft and was selected by the Boston Blades. At the time, I didn't realize that getting picked was a big deal, as all I was focused on was getting back to playing professional hockey—I had just received hip surgery in the spring and was eager to finish rehab and return to the ice.

I'll never forget the day I moved to Boston. My real life in hockey was about to begin, but taking that step was a little scary. Mostly, this was because I had to drive our old 1999 Subaru Outback all the way to Boston. My mom had put a bumper sticker on the back that said "She shoots, she scores," but other than that, the car was a bit worse for wear. It was the vehicle my brothers and I shared, and it had gone through a massive hailstorm, so it was covered with dents. To make matters worse, it had also been keyed. But it always got me where I needed to go . . . despite being an eyesore.

When I arrived in Boston, I was in for a rude awakening. I was living on my own, and now that I was out of school, I didn't have a scholarship to help me financially. The Blades didn't pay, so all I had was my training stipend from the US Olympic committee. I needed to train and be ready for competition, but I wasn't able to make ends meet—most of my meals consisted of toast and peanut butter. I dreamed of winning an Olympic gold medal, but was that even possible?

At Wisconsin, the athletes had close to anything they wanted, and now I was sitting on a couple of old milk crates getting dressed in a community rink bathroom. *What happened?* I thought, looking around. *How did I get here?*

One day I was in a supermarket shopping when I saw the young guy wheeling carts back into the store, and it hit me that he was making more money than I was. A wave of frustration came over me. I called my mom.

My mom has always believed in me. Sharing
the win at the 2017 World Championships
with her was a very special moment for me.

"Mom, I don't know what to do," I cried into the phone. "I don't think I can live in Boston. I can't afford it."

She listened to me, then kindly told me that if I wanted to play hockey, I needed to get a job. My mom wouldn't let me give up—she never had before—and that's when I started taking on extra work to pay my bills. I would drive my old car all the way across Boston to teach a lesson, and then I would have to drive all the way back to my house. After a few weeks of that, it dawned on me that half of the money I was making was going to pay for gas. On paper, it didn't make much sense, but even that little bit of profit kept me afloat. *I guess being a woman and playing professional hockey means going without,* I thought. At the end of the day, I would sacrifice whatever I had to play the game that I loved, and I set my sights on the 2014 Olympics in Sochi.

It was easy to stay motivated going into the games, but the downtime was the hardest part. Our team policies were very strict, and we felt like we were on lockdown most of the time, so we ended up watching Apple TV and the Olympic feed in our rooms. The highlight was "escaping the room" and going to the dining hall for crepes. The low point was watching Canada walk away with another gold medal after battling them in overtime in a game that we dominated until the last six minutes.

Over the next couple of years, the women on the US national hockey team became more and more frustrated with the lack of financial support we needed in order to pursue the game that we loved at an optimal level, and finally we decided that we would lay our careers on the line to get that support. We had won gold at the 2016 world championships and would be defending our title on home soil in 2017—and usually we were in Canada or Europe and had to listen to the boos from the crowd. The tournament in Michigan was going to be a big moment for us, but we weren't interested in playing if we couldn't establish a better future for the sport.

That's what kept us firm in our stance as we waited to hear if USA Hockey would want to help us reshape the future of women's hockey. Three days before the world championships began, they agreed to our conditions, and we took a step in the right direction. We would receive better support and greater access to resources, and a commitment to give the national women's team more exposure in the media. We did it—we were finally going to receive comparable travel stipends and accommodations as the men's team. We were finally being treated as equals.

At that point, playing in the world championships was just a bonus. Even though we'd had time off, our agreement with USA Hockey fueled us, and we made it to the finals, where we would battle against our archrivals: Canada. Our teams had a long history of fighting for first, but we were the defending world champions, and now that we were on home ice, the stakes were even higher. Luckily we had the crowd on our side, and their cheers kept us motivated. We played a tight, controlled game and by the end of the third period, were tied 2–2.

Going into overtime, we didn't need to say anything. We knew what we'd gone through as a group and we knew we were capable of accomplishing great things, on and off the ice.

We got back out and took to the ice with renewed energy. Halfway through overtime, one of Canada's defencemen wound up for a shot, but I blocked it. When I saw my teammate Kendall Coyne streaming down the side, I gave her the puck, then followed her up the ice. She passed it and I took a slap shot. As soon as the puck left my stick I knew it was a good shot, but Canada had a good goalie. Fortunately, the puck tucked right underneath the crossbar and found the netting.

I threw up my hands in relief. "We effing did it!" And I was immediately crushed against the boards by our entire team in a group hug yelling, "We did it!"

We had been days away from losing it all, and to win gold at home—you can't write a better story than that. Our fight was about equality, but we wouldn't have been able to do it without creating a sense of unity within the team and making sure that every player, especially our rookies, felt like she was truly a part of the team. That goal and that win was *ours*.

Our next major competition was the 2018 Winter Olympics in Pyeongchang, and we were determined that it would be the year we would unseat Canada. Our team had never been stronger. Whenever I looked around the dressing room, I thought, *This is a special group of women, these are the type of people you dream to surround yourself with. They have what it takes to be successful.* It didn't matter what was thrown at us, we went out and played. On and off the ice we stood together.

The Olympic experience never gets old. From our reception to our facilities, we are always treated really well. The Olympics are that one time when we are at peace, where we feel that we are exactly where we need to be. Every day, waking up is perfect, because we are living our dreams.

We started out strong, winning our preliminary games against Finland and the Olympic athletes from Russia, but then lost against Canada. That stung, but we decided to treat it as a throwaway game to see where we matched up and how to home in on their tendencies. We knew we would meet them in the finals, just as we had the two previous Olympics.

Meanwhile, we had made a new friend, who quickly became our biggest fan. During a men's hockey game, we met Leslie Jones from *Saturday Night Live*, and we instantly hit it off. At our semifinal game against Finland, she leaned over the players' tunnel as we were walking onto the ice and wished us good luck.

"Hilary!" she screamed. "I love you, Hilary! Have a good game!"

We crushed them 5–0. Up next, Canada.

Two nights before the gold-medal game, I told all three of my brothers—but specifically William, because he's the loudest one—that in a game like this, every little detail matters. "Make sure you guys are cheering loud," I said. "We need USA cheers."

"Of course, Hilary. Go out there and win this thing."

We're going to win, I thought as I laced up my skates the day of the game.

Canada couldn't beat us so many times in a row—we were a strong team, and I knew that our talent would present itself at the right time. We had already showed that we were capable of performing in extraordinary circumstances, and this was no different. While I projected confidence, in the back of my mind, I knew we hadn't won a gold medal in twenty years. We were still the underdogs as far as Olympic gold was concerned.

We went out there and the game unfolded just as we'd thought. The best part? As players and competitors, we utilized all our skill sets on the ice, passing the puck as much as possible, getting as many shots on net as we could, and eliminating odd-man rushes. We started off with a goal in the first period, then Canada scored two in the second. We were a little nervous, but we got more comfortable as the game went on, and on the bench, there was an aura of calm, collective intensity, even as the clock was running out in the third. With minutes to spare, Monique Lamoureux-Morando broke away and scored a goal, tying up the game.

As we so often had in the past, we went into overtime, and when no one scored, we started a shoot-out.

I turned to my teammate Hannah Brandt. Both of us were laughing. "Of course this game would go into a shoot-out."

This was 2014 all over again, but this time we were going to do whatever it took to get that gold. I wasn't tired, and I knew our goalie, Maddie Rooney, was ready. When I looked at her, she had a big smile on her face.

Gigi Marvin started us off with a goal, and in competitive fashion, Canada tied it up. We continued on, back and forth. Again, we were tied. The next goal would determine the winner. I got up but missed my shot, which was upsetting because I knew Maddie would be under more pressure to make a big save. But I had no time to worry, our Jocelyne Lamoureux-Davidson (Monique's twin sister) sunk the puck in the net with her signature shot, faking a right hand wrist shot, going left, then right again. Would the Canadians tie it up? Or miss? We held our breath as we watched from the bench. Meghan Agosta skated towards Maddie and tried to get around her, but Maddie stopped the puck. We had done it!

*With my whole family, Remy, Jamie, my
mom Cynthia, my dad James, and William,
after winning gold at Pyeongchang.*

The entire team jumped off the bench, dropping our gloves and sticks, to meet Maddie with open arms as she came racing towards us. We all fell in a heap on the ice as we realized that we had brought the United States to gold for the first time in twenty years.

"We fucking did it!" we all kept saying.

After we left the rink, we met up with our families to celebrate, though we didn't have much time with them because we were needed on the set of the *Today* show to tape what would be the morning segment back in the United States.

The next few weeks were a whirlwind of media appearances. Throughout our gold-medal game, Leslie had been tweeting a running commentary, calling herself "Penalty Box Jones," and saying that's where she would be if she played hockey. After we won, she told me she wanted us on the show. I grew up watching *SNL*, and it had been on my bucket list to be on the show—and now it was finally happening, and with Penalty Box Jones! But first, we were scheduled to go on *Ellen*. Those media hits were incredible. Ellen teased me about my voice being hoarse from all the yelling and celebrating. Too much champagne will do that! And Leslie made all my *SNL* jitters go away.

We felt like rock stars when we returned from South Korea, and winning gold was a big part of that, but the most rewarding experience was being able to share our win with the people who had always believed in us. For me, that was my mom. She never stopped encouraging me to reach for that gold and I wouldn't be wearing it around my neck if it wasn't for her. But even more importantly, our win meant that we were growing the game for the next generation of women players.

When I show my medal to young girls, their faces light up, and I like to think that they're being inspired to follow their dreams—just as I was when I watched the women's team win gold in 1998. And if their dream includes hockey, hockey will be able to provide for them.

I got a reputation for taking the best selfies after I captured our whole team celebrating our Olympic gold medal. These women are some of the greatest people and greatest hockey players, and it's such a privilege to represent our country alongside them.

They won't have to drive an old beat-up car across a busy city to teach a hockey lesson just to make ends meet.

Hilary Knight is an ice hockey forward with the US national team and the Les Canadiennes de Montreal of the Canadian Women's Hockey League (CWHL), a seven-time world champion, a three-time Olympic medallist, and a CWHL MVP recipient. When she was playing for the Wisconsin Badgers, she held the team record for the most points, goals, and power-play goals in one season. With the Boston Blades, she became the first American-born player to win the CWHL's Most Valuable Player Award and led the team in scoring to win the 2013 Clarkson Cup. In 2018, she was named to Forbes' 30 Under 30 list. Visit her at www.hilary-knight.com or follow her on Twitter and Instagram at @hilaryknight.

Shifting the Culture

Brock McGillis

*When someone asked me what I was going to do with my
life, I said, "Play professional hockey." Hockey was my
future, and nothing could jeopardize that. I was at odds
with myself, and as a result, I suppressed that part of
me that knew I was gay. I lived in denial and in fear.*

I grew up in the small town of Markstay, Ontario, population five
hundred, where my house was right next door to the local rink. My
dad, an Ontario Hockey League (OHL) scout and a junior hockey
coach, knew the owner of the arena personally, and as soon as it
opened each day, I was there, and I stayed until it closed. I was on the
ice at least fifteen times a week, and every Saturday when the teams
from nearby Sudbury came to practice, I'd lug my equipment down
the street in hopes that they needed an extra goalie. My mom and
dad would often show up at the arena with dinner because I wouldn't
leave—that's how much I loved the game.

I wasn't always so keen to be on the ice. In my town and in my
family, everyone played hockey. I started playing hockey as a defenceman when I was six years old, but I wasn't interested in being
out on the rink and would let the other kids take my shifts. When
one of my line mates broke his helmet, I gave him mine. After that,
my dad sat me down.

"You're letting other kids take your ice time, Brock," he said. "Do you not want to play?"

"I do," I replied. "I want to be a goaltender."

"Okay, I'm going to take you to an OHL game and then I want you to tell me three reasons why you want to be a goaltender. Deal?"

"Deal."

We ended up seeing the Sudbury Wolves play the North Bay Centennials. It was my first OHL game, and I took everything in. I watched how the players were on the ice and noticed the reactions they got from the audience and each other. I turned to my dad.

"I have my three reasons," I said.

"All right, what are they?"

"The equipment is cooler, and when the goalie makes a save, everyone cheers for him."

My dad chuckled. "That's all true. What's the third reason?"

"If the team wins, everyone goes to the goalie and congratulates him first." Even at such a young age, I liked the idea of being the player who could make the crowd jump to their feet, the player whom the team relied on to save the day.

"Okay, Brock, we'll get your some goalie equipment," my dad acquiesced.

Once I started playing in net, it was nearly impossible to get me off the ice, but there was a time coming when I would question whether I even belonged in hockey.

I remember it was around the time I started playing hockey that I saw a movie with a gay character. I was always an inquisitive kid, and the character got me thinking.

"Am I gay?" I asked my parents.

They didn't bat an eye. "I'm not sure," my mom said. "But if you are, you are."

I didn't think much more about it then, but as I got older and

*Here I am in my Markstay Bruins
jersey and goalie equipment. This
was my first year playing in net.*

went through puberty, I realized that I was gay. I was fortunate to grow up in a household where there was no homophobia, and if I came out to my parents, they would support me, but I was also part of a larger family—the hockey family. While I considered my teammates to be my friends, I was terrified that they would not accept me.

When I was fourteen years old, playing Bantam hockey, I remember being in the locker room getting ready for a game, and all around me, the guys were bantering as they always did.

"That's gay," one of them said to another player, teasing him about some show of weakness on the ice.

Elsewhere in the room, another conversation was going on, and I heard someone say, "What a homo."

I immediately felt a sense of self-loathing. I knew they weren't directing their comments towards me, but I felt their impact all the same. And their words hurt. These were my friends. Hockey was my life, and I felt that there was no place for someone like me because the sport was about being tough, about being the manliest man, and I knew I would be seen as weak.

But my whole identity was tied up in hockey. I was the kid whose parents would have to drag him off the rink to eat his dinner. When someone asked me who I was, I told them, "I'm a hockey player." When someone asked me what I was going to do with my life, I said, "Play professional hockey."

Hockey was my future, and nothing could jeopardize that. I was at odds with myself, and as a result, I suppressed that part of me that knew I was gay. I lived in denial and in fear. The thought of being exposed crippled me to the point where I couldn't come out to my parents or my young brother Cory, who also played hockey. What if they heard homophobic language and confronted the person who spoke? Would that out me? I couldn't risk that happening, and so I told no one my secret.

I lied about who I was and began dating as many girls as I could. If I so much as thought about a man, I got angry with myself and became depressed. I felt like a fraud and drew away from my team-mates to avoid them seeing through my ruse.

My fear fueled me to play my best. *If I'm good, no one will bother me,* I rationalized to myself. I still felt the most joy when I was on the ice, and ironically, hockey became my lone sanctuary, a place where I could forget my secret and escape the constant dread. But as soon as I stepped off the ice, that feeling of freedom vanished.

It wasn't long until my internal struggle began to manifest in other ways. When I was fifteen, I broke my hand defending myself from someone at school who called me gay. That same year, I was drafted by the Windsor Spitfires of the OHL, which was and remains one of the happiest moments of my life, because I had achieved this milestone while I was only in Midget AAA. And I'd been able to conceal who I really was. But that pressure to hide only increased. In the OHL, I had to have a girlfriend, and she had to be someone who my teammates thought was attractive. As I played my year in the juniors, I struggled to keep up appearances. I felt empty and alone, and I drank to forget.

And my body began to betray me. I started with the Spitfires when I was seventeen, and not long after, my hand was skated over during a game. Midway through my first season, I contracted mono, and as I was recovering, I was traded to the Sault Ste. Marie Greyhounds. While there, I had my hand skated over; then later in the year, I injured my meniscus (a piece of cartilage) in my left knee. At

Taking a break during one of my first OHL games with the Windsor Spitfires before my hand injury.

the next training camp I tore my MCL, a ligament in my right knee. A player was on a breakaway, and when he faked a shot, I started to do a butterfly, dropping to my knees to block him. He then tried to deke to my blocker side, and as I extended my leg I felt a pop. The injury forced me to sit out the entire next year.

I was twenty when I returned to the ice with the Kalamazoo Wings, and almost immediately suffered an injury and missed three months of the season. Within three weeks of coming back, I suffered a severe concussion and was benched for the following season. After I recovered, I started playing pro minor hockey in Europe, and as was becoming so often the case, I tore my meniscus—in my right knee this time—during the season. At the time, I shrugged it off as part of the game. Now I know my injuries were psychosomatic, the physical manifestation of my deep depression.

Whenever I had to take time away from the ice to recover, my mental health deteriorated further because I had nothing to escape into. By the time I was twenty-three, the injuries, the fears, the rehab, and the secrets all seemed like too much, and I didn't see a point in living. *You need to figure yourself out*, I told myself. I had to face who I was, but I didn't know how. How could I be gay and play the game I loved? It was then that I accepted myself as a gay man after so long of suppressing my identity and masking it with girlfriends and alcohol.

I began going out with men in Toronto, a place where I felt I could be anonymous without being outed in the hockey community, and I met someone whom I started seeing seriously. But I was so paranoid of being found out, I used an alias when I was with him and his friends, and I refused to let him meet anyone in my life. In hindsight, I should have reached out to my supportive family, but we were all so tied up in the community, I couldn't bring myself to say anything, because I still wanted to make it as a pro hockey player. I was ranked fairly high on the NHL draft list and my career was supposed to go a certain way, and with my injuries, I couldn't afford any setbacks.

In 2008, I had been with my boyfriend for almost two years when I went to play university hockey at Concordia in Montreal. I told him that I might have to date women to keep up appearances. What a thing to say to someone you love. I wish I could take that back now—it still hurts to think of how badly I wanted approval from a world that didn't approve of me. Not long after I moved, that relationship ended.

Right out of training camp, I retore the meniscus in my right knee and sat out the season. The next year, I was back playing on the team, though my knee was still giving me problems. I was still a part of the team, but most team nights would end with me sneaking off to the Gay Village, although I never made friends whom I could talk to about what I was going through. But that was about to change.

In November 2009, I was watching the Leafs game on TSN, and during one of the breaks, the host began interviewing the Toronto Maple Leafs' president and general manager, Brian Burke, and his son, Brendan. Brendan spoke about following in his father's footsteps and becoming an NHL executive, and then he said he was gay.

Holy shit. I was stunned. No one in the hockey community had ever come out publicly, and here was the son of one of the most powerful NHL executives broadcasting his sexuality and advocating for inclusion within the game.

I immediately reached out to Brendan. Hockey is a small world, and we had enough people in common that when I found him on Facebook, I wasn't a random person in his mind. I told him that I was gay, too, and that I felt like an outsider. It was a relief to share this with someone who understood exactly what I was going through.

Brendan and I quickly became friends. We could talk about anything—my relationship, hockey, and it didn't have to be one or the other. Finally, I felt like I wasn't alone, that there was someone who knew me for who I really was.

Brendan wanted to change the game, to eliminate the homophobia, and he inspired me to do the same. We often talked about how he would make it as a general manager and I would make it as a player. Together we'd break down barriers.

Just a few months after we connected, Brendan was killed tragically in a car accident. Two days before he died, we had exchanged messages on Facebook and he wrote, "I can't wait until the day that you're out like I am." When I had read that, I had panicked at the very thought—I didn't know how to respond, and I didn't get a chance to. Those were his last words to me.

Brendan was the only person who knew my secret, and he was gone. I grieved alone, thinking over that last message. It was time.

I decided to come out to my family, and I started with my brother, a first round OHL pick, a hypermasculine left winger who wasn't afraid to get into fights and scored a lot of goals. I was worried how he was going react, but when I told him, the first thing he said was, "Yeah, so?"

I was in disbelief. My brother was a macho man, and he accepted me without a second thought. He went on to tell me that he loved me, and that he didn't care that I was gay. It didn't change anything between us.

Later that summer, I told my parents, but I think my dad already suspected. After all, in the last three years, I'd gone from being the hockey guy who had regrettably been a bit of a womanizer, to dating no women. Both my mom and dad were very supportive.

"We wish you could have told us earlier," my dad said.

"But we understand what must have held you back," my mom added.

Their words meant so much to me, and it was a relief not to have to hide who I was from my family, but I still kept my sexuality a secret from everyone else, especially my teammates.

Around the time of Brendan's accident, I had left Concordia to move back home and go to Laurentian University. I tried to get back on the ice, but I could barely play. I had no cartilage left in either knee and I was in constant pain every time I skated. After a few months, I decided to leave university hockey and play professionally in the United States. Thanksgiving weekend, I drove eight hours from Sudbury all the way to the Canada-US border in Windsor, and just as I was about to fill out the paperwork to get a visa, I stopped myself. *What the hell am I doing?* I thought. *Why am I so bent on playing hockey when it hurts to even skate?*

"I'm done with hockey," I said to myself. The statement liberated me.

I turned my car around, drove to Toronto, and went out in the Gay Village, and for the first time, I felt free from all judgement. I let my former life go and allowed my new one to begin.

Over the next couple of years, I finished school and began working with athletes in Sudbury, helping them with on-ice and off-ice training and coaching players who were looking to advance to the OHL or the NCAA. I never divulged my sexuality to any of the athletes, because I thought that parents and kids wouldn't want to work with me. Still, I was always quick to shut down any homophobic language used in my presence.

One day, a hockey mom called me up and told me that she wanted to set me up on a date.

"Okay," I said, rolling my eyes. "What's her name?"

"Steve," she answered.

I must have misheard. "What?"

"His name is Steve."

I wasn't about to come out to this hockey mom over the phone, so I asked her what she was talking about.

"Brock, you're gay." She sounded like she was getting a little frustrated.

"How do you know that?"

"My son told me. All the boys know," she said. "They've known for years."

I started to panic. *These players are very masculine*, I thought. *They're not going to want to work with me anymore.* Then what she said sank in. The boys had known for a while and they'd chosen to work with me anyway. The realization that they had accepted me really hit home.

I decided to do an experiment and observe the players' behaviour more closely. I began to notice that whenever they used homophobic language, they froze and apologized to me.

"It's no big deal," I'd say.

More and more, this became the standard reaction. *It must be because they know me and like me*, I thought. *They don't want to offend me.*

A short while later, a coach called me.

"You'll never believe what happened today," he said. He went on to explain.

At the end of a workout that day, the coach had told the players to do a strenuous drill, and one of the boys had replied, "That's so gay."

An older kid spoke up and said that his comment was not okay. The boy agreed, and when the coach told him to do fifty push-ups, he did them without complaining.

As I listened to the story, I realized that a shift had occurred. I hadn't even been there with the team, but just from the boys knowing me, they had started to act and respond differently. That was encouraging.

While the players whom I worked with and their families accepted me, I still didn't feel I needed to come out more publicly. Word did spread, though, and I found myself being blackballed from working with certain teams. That's when I realized that I couldn't let anyone use my sexual orientation against me. After the horrifying shooting at the Pulse nightclub in Orlando, Florida, I knew I had to do something, so in November 2016, I decided to come out publicly in a piece for Yahoo! Sports and start the dialogue for change. I've never felt as strong as I did when I was writing my story. While I was nervous as it hit the press, I was also incredibly confident and empowered.

The response was overwhelmingly positive, and people throughout every league reached out to offer me their support. There was also a backlash. People whom I once considered friends no longer spoke to me. The older generation, in particular, has been less

Nowadays I spend my time training athletes at the Junior A and OHL level. This shot was taken after a day of drills at the Sudbury Arena. (Left to right: Matty Mayhew, Damien Giroux, Brett Jacklin, me, Brad Chenier, and Dan Walker.)

accepting, and others still perpetuate homophobic beliefs and be- haviours. It's been challenging being one of the first out people in the hockey community, but that has made the reward even greater.

I still get to work with athletes and help them realize their dreams of making it to the OHL and NCAA, but I've also started partnering with schools across Canada, hockey teams and associations, and the OHL to create awareness. The dialogue must be changed, and every- one—players, coaches, management, and parents—has a part to play, because homophobic words have been passed down through genera- tions. Think about it: Many hockey hopefuls leave home at a young age, and the game is all they know. That indirect language, that hockey slang, is all they hear. With the help of Brian Burke, and Patrick Burke, Brendan's brother, slowly but surely, we're breaking that cycle.

While youth today are much more progressive and open to play- ing with gay athletes, we still haven't seen a professional hockey player come out during their career, and that needs to change. Hockey will be better for it. My goal is to shift the culture. As a kid, there was noth- ing I wouldn't do to get on the ice, and I want to make sure that the rink, the bench, and the locker rooms are a safe and happy place, that all people can play the game they love without worry of judgement or ridicule, because they'll know they're not alone. I'll never forget how Brendan was there for me, and I hope I can be there for others, too.

Brock McGillis is a former OHL and professional hockey player and has played in both the United States and Europe. He cur- rently works as a mentor and provides on- and off-ice training for elite-level hockey players. An influential advocate for the LGBTQ+ community, he speaks at schools, businesses, and confer- ences and provides inclusivity training for companies. He splits his time between Sudbury and Toronto. Follow him on Instagram at @b_rock33 or on Twitter at @brock_mcgillis.

The Quiet Champion

Kevin Monkman

Hockey and coaching are in my blood, and I've discovered that if you love something, it never feels like work.

Hockey is a staple of small-town Canada, and you can't get much more small-town than Vogar, Manitoba, the tiny Métis community where I grew up. A single road cuts down the middle of the town and features one store, one school, one baseball diamond, and one outdoor rink. There isn't much to do in or around Vogar—it's over 150 kilometres from Winnipeg—so in the summer, we kids were at the baseball diamond, and in the winter, at the rink. That was my favourite time of the year, because it meant playing hockey with my friends. My grandpa had put me on skates when I was very young, and I fell in love with the game and the friendships that came with being a part of a team.

"Going to get some drills in, Mom!" I would yell every morning the temperature was below zero.

"Just make sure you're on time for school," she'd call back. She liked that hockey was keeping me busy and active.

"I will!"

We lived next door to the rink and the school, where my mom taught, so I was always out on the ice before *and* after school, practicing my crossovers and snap shots. Only my mom calling me for dinner could interrupt me.

As soon as I finished eating, I would head right back out. Technically, the rink was only for the teenagers in the evenings, but I would sneak out there and work on my puck-handling skills until the lights turned off at nine p.m.

When I wasn't on the ice, my favourite thing to do was spend the day at my grandparents' house. Almost every Saturday, I was over at their place, and my routine never varied: I ate pancakes in the morning, hauled firewood for the stove in the afternoon, and after dinner, watched the first period of *Hockey Night in Canada* with my papa. Then it was time for my own *Hockey Night in Canada* in the kitchen, where the table was perfectly positioned to be the net for my private game of hockey with my ministick and rubber ball. The night always ended with me winning the Stanley Cup and eating a piece of cake or pie that my grandmother had made.

I didn't have to play ministicks by myself for long. When I was five, my brother Wade was born, and as soon as he was old enough, we played hockey together. I still took every opportunity I could to practice my skills, whether it was in my grandparents' kitchen or out on the ice. From a young age, I saw how hard my parents worked, my mom as a teacher and my dad as a track supervisor for the Canadian National Railway, to provide for me, Wade, and my older brother, Kelly, and older sister, Elaine. I strove to do the same, putting in the hours on the ice in the hopes that one day I would play on a real team in a real league.

When I was seven, my parents signed me up for Novice hockey in Ashern, a thirty-minute drive east of Vogar. Three of my cousins were on the same team as me, so our parents and grandparents would take turns driving us to Ashern for practices and games. We were often rushed for time and had to dress in our gear in the back of the car on the way there, which was no easy feat, not to mention

Here I am, in the front row, fourth from the left, with my Ashern novice team celebrating our win at a tournament in Eriksdale, Manitoba. When I told my son about getting dressed in the car on the way to the rink, he thought it was a funny story until he had to do the very same thing on the way to one of his playoff games.

uncomfortable. But we never minded. We were just happy to be wearing official jerseys.

When our coach gave them to us, he said, "You're part of a team now, and a team only works when all the players have each other's back. Be proud of how you play, because you'll always be remembered by the number on your jersey."

I took that advice to heart. Every practice, I did everything I could to get to the same level as our team's best players. Every game, I strove to outplay and outmaneuver my opponents while still protecting my teammates. When people saw my jersey number, I wanted them to see a power forward who was willing to leave it all on the ice for his team.

My grandpa and my mom always kept me focused on playing my best, too. They never missed a game, and if I wasn't performing as well as I could, I'd feel a tap on my helmet when I was coming off the ice between periods. That was my mom's way of saying, "You need to pick up your game."

After a few years, my dad's work brought him to Dauphin, about an hour and a half away, and we then split our time between Vogar, where my mom still taught, and Dauphin. When I was twelve, my mom was offered a teaching job in Peguis, and my parents decided that Wade and I would move with her, and we would visit my dad, Kelly, and Elaine on the weekends. It was hard being spread across the province, but we made it work, and as always, I had hockey to think about. Peguis is the largest First Nations community in the

During my season with the Peguis Bantams, I played in the Manitoba Indigenous Cultural Education Centre hockey tournament and received the MVP trophy, which then Judge Murray Sinclair presented to me.

province, with over ten thousand people of Ojibway and Cree descent, and it was by far the biggest city I'd ever played in. I was a little intimated at first, but after my first season in Pee Wee, I realized there was nothing to worry about.

"Nice work out there," my coach said after a game. "You've got soft hands, and you're still playing a physical game."

"Thanks, Coach," I replied. "I've been practicing."

"It shows. Keep playing like that."

By the time I was fifteen, I was competing for a spot on the Parkland Rangers, an AAA team in Dauphin, against some of the best players I'd seen. Fortunately, I made the cut. *One step closer to Junior A*, I told myself.

I moved to Dauphin and stayed with my dad and older siblings. Wade still went to school and played hockey in Peguis, but if he didn't have a game on the weekend, he and my mom would drive the two and a half hours to Dauphin on Saturday morning to see us before heading back on Sunday night.

My papa still drove to Dauphin from Vogar to attend my games, but even though he and my dad were often with me, I felt like I was a long way from my home, my friends, and my community in Peguis. Hockey was the only constant, and the competition was much tougher in Dauphin. *Just one more reason to throw myself into the game*, I thought. As the season progressed, I discovered that the more time I spent on the ice, the less homesick I felt.

After one of my games, an RCMP officer asked to speak with number 29. That was me. I wore twenty-nine after my favourite player, Gino Odjick.

My first thought was that I was in trouble, but that was ridiculous—I was just playing hockey. Still, I was apprehensive when I met the officer outside the locker room.

"Number 29?" he asked, extending his hand.

"That's me." I shook his hand. "Kevin Monkman."

"Kevin, I've been watching you all season," he said. "You're talented. You give everything you have to the game. You're tough, but fair. I think you'd be a good fit for our summer student program."

"Oh, thank you." I let out a breath I hadn't realized I was holding. That wasn't what I had expected to hear. *I guess my Novice coach was right*, I thought. *People know you by the number on your back.*

He went on to explain that another student and I from Dauphin would attend a two-week training course, be issued a uniform, and accompany officers on all their calls. "Would you be interested in joining us this summer?"

"Yeah, I think that sounds fun."

I was getting noticed inside and outside the hockey world. As my first year with the Parkland Rangers rounded out, Dauphin began to feel more like my home—I was making friends and playing well—and I started to imagine what it might be like to join the local Junior A team, the Dauphin Kings, once I was eligible. Kelly had played a few games with the Kings, and the first time my dad took me to see them, I was in awe. I still remember walking into the arena. I was so impressed with how fast the players were. *I want to be a King*, I thought. *Someday I'll play for them, too.*

But that summer, my coach told me that the Selkirk Steelers, another Junior A team almost four hours away, had selected me. While I was happy to be in the juniors, I was secretly hoping to somehow make it to the Kings, not just because I thought they were a stronger team, but because Dauphin was closer to my biggest fan: my papa.

Before I moved up to the juniors, I had one more year with the Rangers, during which the Kings asked Hockey Manitoba if they could borrow me just for their playoffs. Hockey Manitoba agreed. I was thrilled and determined to play my best.

Luckily, I had one of the best coaches out there—Lyle Stokotelny.

He had played for the Kings and won the Manitoba Junior Hockey League (MJHL) championship in 1977. He was a tough player back then, and he was a tough coach in the nineties. The Kings hadn't won a championship in a decade, and Lyle took it upon himself to rebuild the team and get us to the playoffs.

He was a straight shooter who had no problem telling us how things were, and we needed his guidance because we were still such a young team. I was always impressed by his ability to get the absolute best out of us.

"I know Dauphin's a small town, but I don't want to hear about any partying," he told us. "If you don't commit yourself to this team and come to every practice and every game ready to give your all, you can say goodbye to winning the championship."

He had our attention. All of us wanted to win that trophy, and we did everything he said.

"Just keep your head in the game," he'd say in the locker room. "We're going to take this shift by shift."

We started out with a bang, crushing the Winkler Flyers in the opening round, then knocking off the Portage Terriers, who were by far the best team of the league that year.

"There's no stopping you," Lyle told us in the dressing room as we prepared to meet Saint Boniface in the finals. "Focus on the task at hand, and you'll walk out of here with that trophy."

And we did. As I hoisted the Turnbull Cup over my head, I couldn't help but think how far we'd come as a team and how far I'd come as a player to be celebrating this win with the Kings in front of my family in the stands.

I'm sure Lyle said some thoughtful words to us in the dressing room afterwards, but all I remember is the champagne flying and burning my eyes. There's no doubt we would not have won without our coach, though, and when the call went out for MJHL Coach of the Year nominations, we put Lyle forward. It was the least we could do to show our appreciation for everything he had done for us. He ended up tying for the award.

I didn't know it at the time, but the lessons Lyle taught us— lessons about commitment and teamwork—would serve me well when I began coaching years later.

After we won the championship, I thought maybe I would be traded to the Kings, but that summer I got the news that I had been traded to the Southeast Blades, who were based in Winnipeg, just as far away as the Steelers. I was crushed. The move from Peguis to Dauphin had been tough at first, and at seventeen years old, I wasn't looking forward to living in a big city where I had no friends.

Fortunately, I had a cousin playing with the Blades, and we were pretty close, so I arranged to billet with his family, which made the idea of moving a lot easier. I think Wade was a little too happy to see me go. Twenty minutes after I left Dauphin, he had already moved into my room! Still, for a good month, I wished I was back home, but the hockey made me change my mind. Playing on the same line as my cousin was fun, and we were good.

I don't know what I would have done without my family. Whenever they could, they came to see my games in Winnipeg, and if I was playing closer to home, my papa would make it there. Behind the scenes, I knew my parents were making sacrifices for me to stay in hockey. As a teacher, my mom was supposed to have summers off, but she took a job one summer to help pay for my hockey fees and equipment, and my dad was a tireless worker even after he finished his day with the CN. In the summers, he would always make sure our grass was cut and our yard looked good, and in the fall and winter, he cut firewood for our woodstove. Their commitment to my hockey career motivated me to play my best even when other players weren't so friendly.

When we played in bigger cities, I'd sometimes hear an opposing player say something racist during a game. I was called "chief" and "wagon burner," among other hateful slurs. Somehow I kept my focus while the game was on, but afterwards, their words stuck with me. I'd remember the jersey number of the player who had said those things, and in the next game, I'd make him pay, whether that was with a choice check or by stealing the puck away. Showing my superiority on the ice was my way of combating their ignorance.

In 1993, I was starting my second season with the Southeast Blades when my coach, who knew I missed being in Dauphin, told me that they had traded me to the Kings.

"Are you serious?" I asked.

"We'll miss you, Kevin," he said, smiling. "But I know you'll do well there, too."

I was over the moon to return to Dauphin. I'll never forget my first game back home. I was put on a line with Riley Wallace and Lars Molgard, and it was instant chemistry. *This is where I'm meant to be*, I thought.

I played with the Kings for another three seasons, and as my time in the juniors began to close out, I started to think seriously about my career. As much as I loved playing hockey competitively, I knew that junior was as far as I was going to go. I wanted hockey to stay in my life, but I wasn't sure what that would look like. After I played my last game in Dauphin, I did some work as an assistant coach with the Blades, but my priorities began to shift from hockey to family. You see, I had gotten married, moved to Winnipeg, and had a daughter, Deana.

I wanted to provide stability for my family, so I went back to school for a diploma in business administration and found work as a research analyst for Manitoba Hydro. While I continued to coach casually part-time, I focused on my new job and being a father. Four years after Deana was born, Jenna came along, and five years after that, Kevin Jr. arrived.

Family always came first, but little did I know that a new opportunity to coach was also around the corner. I was at the 2012 Red River Exhibition with my kids when I ran into Dale Bear, a young guy I had coached with the Peguis Juniors, a Junior B team.

"Dale," I said, shaking his hand. "Long time no see. How are you doing?"

"It's been a while," he said. "It's so good to see you. Are these your kids?"

"Yeah, this is Deana, Jenna, and Kevin Jr."

"Nice to meet you, guys. Did you know your dad used to coach me?"

They shook their heads.

"Dale," I asked. "What have you been up to?"

"I'm coaching, believe it or not. Right now I'm with our provincial women's team for the National Aboriginal Hockey Championships."

I remembered that the NAHC was just getting started when I was coaching Dale. I'd always thought it was an amazing initiative—the NAHC is an annual tournament for Indigenous hockey players across Canada. Manitoba typically sends one men's and one women's team of athletes from fourteen to eighteen years old.

"Oh, man, that's fantastic. Good for you. You must be busy."

"I am." He paused. "Actually, I'm glad I ran into you, Kevin."

"Why's that?"

"The NAHC is looking for a coach for Manitoba's men's team. Are you interested?"

I looked down at my kids. I didn't want to commit myself to something that would take me away from them, but I believed in what the NAHC was doing for Indigenous youth. I thought of all the invaluable lessons coaches had taught me over the years, and the idea of giving back and mentoring the next generation of players stirred something inside me. *It wouldn't too time-consuming*, I thought. *I'd be coaching for a single championship, not an entire season.*

I turned back to Dale. "Sure, I'll look into it," I replied.

And with that, I dipped one toe back in the coaching pool. Not long after, I dove in headfirst. I began coaching the men's team and scouting players from across Manitoba to join it. Once again, I was in the world of minor-league hockey, and I loved it. I had missed being at the rink and leading a team, and now that I was a father, I felt I had more to offer my players than just hockey plays. I could offer them advice on how to be a champion off the ice, too.

In 2017, the men's Team Manitoba won gold at the NAHC championships for the first time since the tournament's inaugural year. I was proud to be a part of their victory.

I was heading into my third NAHC with Team Manitoba when Bruce Sinclair, the GM of the Peguis Juniors, gave me a call. I didn't know Bruce, but I had coached some of his players in the NAHC.

"Kevin," he said. "I'm looking for a coach for the Peguis Juniors, and I immediately thought of you."

"I don't know, Bruce," I replied. "Peguis is a two-hour drive from here. I'm not sure I have the time right now to coach a team week after week for an entire season."

"I know it's a lot to ask. But you know most of these players already. Didn't you used to play there, too? It would be the perfect fit."

While raising my kids had always been a priority, I had recently divorced, and I had to weigh the pros and cons of taking on such a big commitment. *How would the kids feel about me being away more?* I thought.

"Kevin? You there?"

"I'm here. Listen, I really appreciate the opportunity, but I have to talk to my kids first."

"You do what you need to. Let me know what you decide."

I hung up the phone and went to find my children.

"Hey guys," I started. "I want to run something by you and get your opinion."

"Sure, Dad," Deana said. "What's up?"

Jenna and Kevin looked at me expectantly, and I filled the three of them in on Bruce's offer. "What do you think? Should I take the job?"

"You love coaching, Dad." Deana smiled. "You should go for it."

The other two nodded.

"Okay, I will." I gave them each a hug. "I love you, guys."

I called Bruce back and told him that I would coach the Peguis Juniors, but just for a year to see how it went. Deana was eighteen by then and agreed to be home with Jenna and Kevin while I was coaching. I knew balancing work, family, and coaching would be difficult, but I was excited by the challenge in front of me.

That first day of practice, I hopped in my van and drove the two hours from my house in Winnipeg to Peguis. On the drive up, I thought through the game plan for the season. I knew that a devastating fire in 2007 had destroyed the team's arena. They'd had a rough go, but with generous funding from the province, a first-class arena had been built a few years ago. The Peguis Juniors had a home once more, and I was determined that this was going to be their year.

The team had won the Keystone Junior Hockey League (KJHL) championship just four times since 1994. Their most recent win was the previous year, so I knew they had what it took to be champions, and I wanted to help them rise to the next level. There is no national championship for Junior B hockey in Canada, but if the team could win their league, they would have a chance to represent Manitoba in the Western Canadian Junior B Championship and earn the title of the best Junior B team in Canada. A Manitoba team had never won before.

I had learned from my days with the Kings playing for Lyle that the most important thing to get from your players is commitment. The number of Xs and Os I drew on the play board wouldn't matter unless the players were giving 100 percent. And that was going to be my philosophy for Peguis. I had goose bumps just walking into that facility. This was a new beginning for the team and for me. I could feel it.

Bruce was there to greet me and introduce me to the team. I nodded at the familiar faces in the locker room and said a few words.

"I'm thrilled to be coaching you all this year," I started. "All I ask of you guys is to be here, to work hard, and to compete, really compete, every night. When you step on that ice, you're coming to work. If you do that, you will always give yourself the opportunity to win."

I looked around the room and the boys were all nodding.

"Okay, let's get out there then." And that was it. We had a terrific practice, and on the drive back to Winnipeg, I knew I had found a coaching home. The people of Peguis had always been passionate about hockey—I knew that from when I used to play there—and these players were no different. I felt like I could see myself in them.

In the following weeks, I got to know the boys on my team better, and there were a few players who stood out. One was Quinton Flett. I had watched him play when I was scouting for Team Manitoba and been blown away. He was one of those players who, if they brought it every night, were unstoppable. And he brought it most nights. In thirty-three games, he had thirty-three goals and seventy-three points.

The team played pretty well together, but our defence needed some work. We were winning games, but by close margins. It helped that we picked up Luke Penner from the OCN Storm. He was incredible in net and a big part of ensuring our victories, but the team needed to work more cohesively. We couldn't rely on our rookie goalie Dray Flett to save us every night. So, after the Christmas break, we focused on tightening up our defence not through any specific drill, but by changing our mind-set. Scoring eight goals in one night was great, but we needed to commit to playing better in our end. Once we did that, we started winning games 5–2 or 5–1. I liked those margins.

As the season rolled on, I began to realize just how much I was asking from the boys when I gave my speech on commitment. A lot of my players worked or took evening classes, and some of them already had families, so making it out to every practice was difficult. And yet they never failed to show up. They always found the time to come out and work hard for me. And I made sure to tell them how much I appreciated their work ethic, but the results of their efforts spoke louder than my words ever could. Off the ice, they were pursuing their education and job opportunities, and on the ice, they were dominating.

Still, our road to the KJHL championship was hard. The team finished the regular season fifth in the league and got hot just as we entered the playoffs. We were up against the Selkirk Fishermen first. The boys gave everything they had, and we defeated them in just four games. But we weren't out of the woods yet. We went on to play the St. Malo Warriors, and the whole series was a grind. It took us all seven games to knock them out. We ran with the energy from that series win and swept the Arborg Ice Dawgs in six tough games to win the championship, on home ice no less.

After the final buzzer sounded, the entire bench flooded the ice, swarming the players on the last shift. I was bursting with pride. As I watched them hoist the Baldy Northcott Trophy, I couldn't help but think of my own championship win with the Kings just twenty-three years earlier. I hoped that this victory would show my players a new way to define successes in their own lives, that perseverance and hard work pays off.

But our work wasn't done. The Western Canadian Junior B Championships awaited us. We faced off against the Ice Dawgs in the first game, but we couldn't manage a win, which was frustrating especially since we had just beaten them in our league finals. We secured a victory against the Nipigon Elks, but with the exception of one tie, we lost our last three games. Finishing fifth was hard to take after such a successful league win, but the team members resolved that they would return. And so would I. I was dead tired, but when Bruce asked me to come back the next year, I said yes without hesitating.

From the very start of the 2017–2018 season, we set our sights on winning not just our league, but also the Western Canadian Junior B Championships. Our players, returning and new, were disciplined and committed, and I heard them repeating some of the coaching advice I had given them to each other.

"Stay committed. Stay focused."

We finished the regular season in second place and headed into the league playoffs, where we were up against the North Winnipeg Satelites. Nothing could stop us, and we defeated them in just three games. We continued our winning streak through semifinals against the Lundar Falcons. We were on a roll.

"We have what it takes to win." I reminded the team before we took the ice against the St. Malo Warriors. "We have our game plan."

It took us five games, but we beat them. The Peguis Juniors were champions three years running and for the sixth time in team history. We were on our way to the Western Canadian Junior B Championships in Thunder Bay, Ontario.

The championships are a five-day tournament—every game counts, but I was confident that we were going to play in the finals. We started the round robin against the Thunder Bay Fighting Walleye, a team from a league we had never competed with before, so we were a little intimidated and they didn't cut us any slack. We lost 7–2.

The boys shook off the loss and focused on playing our brand of hockey in our next game, against the Thunder Bay Northern Hawks. They were the best in their league, which was exciting. We had the chance to really show them what we were made of—speed, skill, and brawn. It was a hardscrabble game and we fought for every goal. In the end, we lost 6–5, but we were happy with our performance. The Hawks were a bit older and more experienced, and we had given them a run for their money.

Still, we had started out slow and we needed to win our next two games if we were to have a shot at the Keystone Cup. Fortunately, our last game of the round robin was against the St. Malo Warriors. We'd just defeated them in our league championship two weeks earlier and knew exactly what to do to come out ahead, which we did, 8–1.

We were on to the semifinals, facing off against the Fighting Walleye once more, but we went in confident, knowing what adjustments we needed to make to beat them. We won 6–3. As I predicted, we had made it to the finals, but so had the Northern Hawks. All we had to do was knock out the best team in northern Ontario and we would be number one in western Canada.

Before the final game, I gathered the team in the dressing room.

"You should all be extremely proud of the work you've done, not just in this tournament, but all year." I looked around at the eager faces. "I know you've sacrificed so much this season to come out every practice and every game. You can do this. Let's just take it shift by shift, game by game."

"Yeah!" they cheered.

The boys played hard, but we couldn't get ahead of the Hawks. By the end of the first period, they were up 3–1, and they added another in the second. Luke was doing his best to defend our net and we traded goals in the third, but it wasn't enough. The Hawks won 5–2.

While we had wanted to win it all, it had been a long season and we had played well throughout, setting a team record for consecutive KJHL wins, so we were happy to come out second overall. And Luke was named the top goaltender of the tournament.

I don't usually say much after games—I like to let the guys celebrate or commiserate among themselves—but a few of the players were aging out of the junior category and this had been their last league game. I wanted them to know what a great job they had done that year.

"Congratulations on playing such a strong last season," I said. "For those of you coming back next year, be ready to go."

Assistant coach Marty Favel and I are posing for
a photo with Theron Spence, Tyler Woodhouse,
Devin Garson, and Waylon Nault at the
Western Canadian Junior B Championships.
It was a bittersweet moment because the boys
had just finished their last junior game.

I'm still coaching the Peguis Juniors today. I am so proud of my players, and I try to promote them as much as possible. Over the last couple of years, I've had my eye on Allan Kohli, a young goalie from Winnipeg who was never really given a shot at being the number one net minder. I selected him for two of our NAHC tournaments, and he killed it between the pipes both times. In 2016, when Manitoba won bronze, he was awarded Best Goaltender, and in 2017, he backstopped us to a gold medal. He now plays for me on the Peguis Juniors, where he's one of the top goalies in the league.

The nice thing about winning is that my boys are being noticed.

We have scouts from the Saskatchewan Junior Hockey League and some Ontario Junior A teams come out and look at our players. I tell the boys that it doesn't matter if they live in Vogar, Ashern, Peguis, or Winnipeg—if they're successful, the scouts will find them.

I don't stick around the arena long after practices and games, because I need to get back to my kids in Winnipeg. I spend a good eight hours a week in my van, but the driving isn't a burden. Hockey and coaching are in my blood, and I've discovered that if you love something, it never feels like work. Coaching the young men of the Peguis Juniors, motivating them, instilling discipline in their lives, and bringing out the best in them, is the ultimate gift. I have had the chance to speak with some parents, and they've told me how their kids are excited not only about being a part of the team, but also to head to university and start their careers. Hearing those words is a bonus, but I'm not looking for a pat on the back. All I want is for my guys to play hard. If one of my kids goes on to the NHL, that would be awesome, but if they keep playing hockey, give back to their community, and live a good life, that would be just as awesome.

Besides, hockey isn't a "look-at-me" sport, it's a "we" sport. It's about the friendships that come from being on a team. I've made life-long friends with guys I played with, and even if we haven't seen each other in years, when we do meet up, it's as if no time has gone by and we're back in the dressing room talking about hockey.

Kevin Monkman coaches the Peguis Juniors in the Keystone Junior Hockey League. In 2016, the Manitoba Aboriginal Sports and Recreation Council named him the male Indigenous coach of the year. In November 2017, Global News named him coach of the month. He lives in Winnipeg with his three children.

The Healing Power of Hockey

Pat Kline

*For my dad, hockey was all about being part of a team,
working hard, and celebrating when you had the chance. He
thought about firefighting the same way. "It's about being
there for people when they need you," he would often say.*

In any fire hall in Halifax—or even in Canada—there is always
some hockey talk going on, and the fire halls where my dad, Ray,
worked were no different. He rotated among various fire stations
in Halifax, but whenever he was assigned to our neighbourhood, I
would visit him.

Our home was at the top of Melody Drive and overlooked Bedford Basin, which, according to my grandmother, was always filled
with cargo ships loaded with much-needed supplies for England
during the Second World War. When I was a kid, it was just an easy
ten-minute walk down the hill and along the Bedford Highway to the
fire hall, where the crew would often be rehashing Saturday's hockey
game, my dad listing the follies of the Montreal Canadiens. He was
an ABC, an Anybody But the Canadiens hockey fan. Of course, I was
a huge Habs fan, as was my younger brother Steven, but our differences never came between us, which is funny because from 1965 to
1980, we watched the Canadiens win the Stanley Cup ten times.

We loved hockey in my house. When the city built the Metro

Centre (now the Scotiabank Centre), the whole family—my brothers, Mike and Steven, and my sister Sandy—piled into my dad's big blue 1972 Chrysler Newport, a classic boat of a car, for the Nova Scotia Voyageurs' first game in the new arena. Back then, the team featured Keith Acton and Rod Langway, young players who went on to enjoy long NHL careers. I'll never forget that night, from the drive there with my dad, one hand on the steering wheel, another on his cigarette, to the game in the biggest and best stadium in the Maritimes.

When we weren't gathered around the TV for *Hockey Night in Canada*, we were at the rink, playing hockey or watching my dad referee games for the minor hockey league or the Halifax Fire Department charity tournament.

Ever since I was a young kid, I looked up to my father. Everything he did, I wanted to do, and when I was fourteen, I even started officiating games. My dad was a funny guy and a great storyteller, and

Here's an early photo of my dad in his Halifax Fire Department uniform. He was thirty.

he raised us kids to be good people. If we strayed from the standard he held us to, he would say, "Smarten up, or I'll kick you in the arse!" which got us back in line quickly. Most of all, he was a superhero to me. I remember the day I saw him in action. A fire had broken out in our neighbourhood, and I was in the street, watching him in all his gear focused on quelling the blaze in front of him. *That's what I want to do someday*, I realized.

When I told my dad I wanted to be a firefighter, he gave me a piece of advice. "Your fire crew is just like a hockey team," he said. "You can't win hockey without great teamwork and you can't survive as a firefighter either. You always need to stick up for each other."

I can do that, I thought. I knew that it took time to become a firefighter. As soon as I was done with school, I trained to become an ambulance attendant so that I could develop my skills as a first responder while I started the long process of testing and training to enter the fire department. That was always my end goal.

On December 2, 1981, my dad was called to a garbage fire inside a large shopping complex. The fire was heavy and smoky, and he worked overnight to tame it, ignoring the headache that began to plague him. He assumed it was from the stress of fighting the fire and kept working until his shift ended.

When I came downstairs the next morning, my dad was in the kitchen still wearing his blue work pants and long-sleeve shirt. He was never one to sit around, especially not in his uniform. Whenever he came home from a shift, he got changed right away and made something to eat.

"Dad, are you okay?"

"My head really hurts," he said.

The phone rang. It was Sears, where my dad worked part-time. I covered the receiver with my hand. "Dad, Sears is wondering if you're coming in today. What should I tell them?"

My dad mumbled something about lying down for a few minutes first. Something was off—he was usually on the ball.

"When do you want me to wake you up?" I asked, studying him closely.

He began to count out numbers.

I uncovered the receiver. "I don't think he's going to be able to make it in today," I said, then hung up. "Dad, can you talk to me?" I crossed the kitchen to where he was sitting.

He didn't respond. The room was well lit so I could see that his pupils were dilated. *Has he suffered some kind of brain injury*? I wondered. I immediately went back for the phone and called an ambulance for him. As I waited for the paramedics to arrive, I phoned my mom at work to tell her that Dad was heading to the hospital.

At the time, neither my mom nor I was afraid, because aside from some mild hypertension, my dad had always been in good health. He was just forty-four years old. A firefighter of seventeen years, he was weeks away from becoming a lieutenant. He was indestructible. We both hoped his current disorientation was caused by tiredness and stress. After a few minutes, Tony Godsoe and John Cooper, two medics we knew quite well, arrived, and their familiar presence further reassured me. *There's nothing to worry about*, I thought as I followed the ambulance in my car. *Tony and John are good medics. My dad will be just fine.*

I met my mom at the hospital, and not long after my dad was admitted, the doctor came and told us that my dad had suffered an aneurysm. "We think the stress and the intensity of battling that fire triggered something."

My mom and I were both stunned. "An aneurysm?" she repeated.

"That's the last thing we expected," I said. "He's always been on the go. He's never had any problems before."

"What happens next?" my mom asked, focusing on the doctor.

"When will he recover?" Never a question of "if." That's how much faith we had in my dad.

"It's too soon to tell, but we will be performing surgery to relieve the pressure in his head. Right now, we're monitoring him until the swelling in his brain goes down."

"Can we see him?" I asked.

"Yes, of course. He's still a bit sluggish."

The doctors had to wait a week before they could operate, after which my dad was much more responsive. But when the doctor started asking him questions, we noticed he had problems with his memory.

"Do you know where you are, Ray?"

"I'm in the kitchen at Bedford," he answered, referring to Bedford Road Fire Hall, the first fire station he'd worked at in the sixties.

"No, you're in the hospital," the doctor said. "Do you recognize these people here?" He pointed to me and my siblings.

He did, but he thought we were little kids, not teenagers and young adults. He turned and looked at me. "Pat, make sure you finish your homework before you watch the hockey game."

I think that's the moment that my hope wavered. "Dad, I'm not in school," I said gently. "I work now."

After the doctor finished his evaluation, he told us that our dad's long-term memory was fine—it was his short-term memory that was the problem. They waited another week to see if his memory might return naturally, but it didn't. *He's not going to recovery fully*, I thought. All the things that made him who he was—fighting fires, griping about the Canadiens—were slipping away.

The doctors suggested a second surgery. "It's risky," they said. "But we can try and repair some of the damage." In the operating room, they did the best they could, but the aneurysm had wreaked too much havoc on my dad's brain. The next time I saw him, he was on life support in the ICU, where he remained for three weeks. Two days before Christmas, he passed away.

It's never easy to lose someone you love, but the toughest part for me was not having the chance to say goodbye to him, to tell him I loved him one last time.

I knew my dad was well respected within the firefighting community—he had always been passionate about protecting the rights of his comrades through the union—though I never fully understood his legacy until his funeral. Because he died in the line of duty, he was buried with full department honours, and his fire hall organized a parade for his casket, which they covered with the Canadian flag and placed on top of his old pumper truck. They made sure the pumper drove by Station 7 on Bayers Road, the hall where my dad had worked, on the way to the church. We followed behind in a limo, and as far as I could see, hundreds of firefighters from all over the Maritimes lined the streets and saluted his casket as the pumper went by. I was overwhelmed by the display. *When I become a fire-fighter, I'm joining the honour guard*, I told myself.

At the reception afterwards, my dad's colleagues came up to me and the rest of my family to tell us how fondly they would remember him.

"He was a top-notch firefighter," one of them said. "Always loved a good story."

"Especially if it was about hockey," I replied.

"And he loved his beer!"

"That's true," I said. "Whenever he wasn't working, you could find him with a stubby in hand watching *Hockey Night in Canada.*"

"I hope this doesn't change your mind about becoming a fire-fighter, Pat," another firefighter said.

"Not at all—I'm determined as ever."

"Good," he said, smiling. "We need another Kline."

A few years later, I was still working as an ambulance attendant when the fire department approached my mom about a fund-raising idea.

"We know how much Ray loved hockey," they said. "We thought that hosting a charity hockey tournament would be a good way of honouring his memory and raising money for the Nova Scotia fire-fighters burn treatment society."

"That's a wonderful idea," my mom replied. "What will you call it?"

"The Ray Kline Memorial Hockey Tournament."

"It's perfect."

When I heard the news, I was floored. *Wow*, I thought. *That's the kind of community I'm going to be a part of one day.* Once the tournament was announced, there was no lack of fire halls that wanted to play—Halifax, Dartmouth, Cole Harbour, Sackville—and the owner of Centennial Arena gave them a good deal on the ice time because the previous owner was a friend of my father's. The fire hall even asked if my mom would drop the puck for the opening face-off. Everyone was so thrilled to be part of a charity that meant something to him or her personally. I wasn't with the department that inaugural year, so I volunteered to be a referee, a job I'd been doing for years on the side, just like my dad had.

Soon after, I began my training to become a firefighter. I'd been an ambulance attendant for six years and had learned a lot about what it took mentally to be a first responder. And I was in the best shape of my life, spending fourteen hours a week playing hockey and reffing games. I knew I could pass the physical tests.

At the end of my training, I went in for my board interview with Tommy Abraham, who was an old friend of my dad's. We talked about what it meant to serve the community and the expectations the department had for its firefighters.

"I'm going to work my butt off to be the best firefighter I can

Every year my mom drops the puck at the opening game of the tournament, which is always held in Centennial Arena. This photo is from 2012.

be," I said. "I would never want to tarnish the standard of excellence and teamwork that my dad set." *And if I screwed up*, I thought, *Dad would somehow find a way to kick my arse.*

Tommy closed my file and said, "Pat, don't fail the effing medicals."

I smiled. I was going to make it, and I did.

The day of my graduation, I donned my Halifax Fire Department uniform for the first time. As I stared at my reflection in the mirror, all I could think was, *Dad would have been damn proud of me today.*

When my mom saw me, she had tears in her eyes. "I know it would mean so much to your father to see you following in his footsteps."

"Thanks, Mom."

I queued up with the other newly minted firefighters, and when my name was called, I walked across the stage to receive my badge number. Fire Chief Donald Swan shook my hand, then presented me with my badge. I looked down. It was my dad's badge, number eighteen, that lay in my hand. Blinking back tears, I saluted the chief.

"Congratulations, Pat," he said. "Your dad would be very proud of you."

"Thank you, Chief. I wish he was here for this."

It was a tremendous honour to be given my dad's badge, and from that day forward, I proudly wore the number eighteen on my hat. It became my jersey number in hockey, too. I used to wear number eleven, but after that day, I was eighteen, just like my dad.

As soon as I could, I joined the department's honour guard. Their response to my father's passing, the overwhelming love and support they showed us, had helped our family heal, and I wanted to be sure to give back in any way I could.

But the best thing about being a Halifax firefighter was that I was able to play in the tournament named after my dad. When the game is on, it gets pretty serious, and there are the odd scuffles, but beyond the game itself, the tournament is really a great bonding experience. I was lucky to work with several men whom my dad had worked with, and I lost count of the times these veteran firefighters would tell me how much they respected my dad.

"Ray was always harder on our hockey team than the other fire halls," they'd say, referring to his reffing. "Fighting was never allowed."

"That sounds like him," I'd reply.

In 2016, we decided to start donating the money we raised in the tournament to the Tema Conter Memorial Trust, which supports first responders suffering from post-traumatic stress disorder (PTSD). Tema was a young woman from Halifax who had worked as a fashion buyer in Toronto. Tragically, in 1988, she was brutally murdered. She was just twenty-five. Vince Savoia, one of the first people to respond to the call in Toronto, hadn't been a paramedic for long, but the terrible scene he encountered haunted him for years.

For Vince, part of his recovery was to take action, and he went on to found the trust with Tema's older brother, Howard Conter, who happens to be my family doctor. All the firefighters in Halifax felt for Tema and Howard, and we empathized with Vince, so raising money for the trust was an easy decision.

The presence of PTSD among first responders was and is pervasive. In the past, paramedics or even firefighters didn't speak about it. Even my dad found it difficult. I knew he experienced rough calls, but he rarely talked about them.

"There are certain things I can't tell you, because they are too scary," he'd say, but he would always hasten to add that his crew was there for him. "We depend on each other."

I do remember one time when he was particularly rattled. He told us that he'd responded to a teenage suicide, and the boy was about the same age as my brother Steve. My dad could handle anything, but any call that involved a kid took a toll on him. He was very quiet and we gave him his space as he worked through the trauma that call had been on him. When I became a firefighter myself, I finally understood what he had been going through.

I'm proud to say that the Halifax Fire Department has come a long way from my dad's days, and we now have our own critical-incident team and employee-assistance program to help anyone struggling with PTSD. Still, the biggest challenge of being a firefighter is dealing with the stress that comes from the images we see every time we go to work. We respond to fires and terrible accidents every shift—we see our fair share of death and destruction, and if one of our own is lost, it's a devastating blow for the entire crew. We all have bad days, and we all deal with them in our own way. Sometimes it's through a grim sense of humour, because laughter, even poorly timed, goes a long way to relieve stress. But most of the time, we get by thanks to the support of our crews. The six other people on my shift are my second family, and when something about the job affects me, I talk to them.

I also depend on hockey as much as the crew I work with. Throughout the Halifax-Dartmouth area, there are tons of noon-hour pickup hockey games. I work a twenty-four-hours-on, three-days-off schedule, so I have a lot of opportunities to grab my gear and head to a rink. Sure enough, every time I do, there are three or four other off-duty firefighters playing hockey as well. For that hour that I'm on the ice, I'm not thinking about anything else but the game. I'm focused on my positioning and my defence, and of course, the score. The game consumes me and doesn't let me think about what happened at work twelve hours earlier. Not only is hockey a great way to stay in shape,

In 2015, our fire department won the tournament.
I'm in the second row, second from the left.

it's one of the number one stress relievers for everyone at the fire hall. But the highlight of the year for all of us in Halifax Regional Fire and Emergency is the Ray Kline Memorial Hockey Tournament.

Nova Scotia is known for being the home of some of the NHL's biggest stars, but I think it speaks volumes for our province and the game that our players haven't forgotten their roots. One day, I came into work and there were cameras set up at our fire station.

"What's going on?" I asked.

"We're here to film another safety and training video," one of the camera guys replied.

We had just done an incident-command video three weeks before with the same guys, so I didn't think much of it. But when we started getting on our gear, a van pulled up and out jumped Sidney Crosby and Nathan MacKinnon with Tim Hortons coffee and donuts for everyone. We were stunned.

"Can we hang out with you guys for a while?" Sidney asked.

"Yeah, of course!" we said.

We showed them around the fire hall and let them put our gear on. They were surprised how hard it was to climb a few flights of stairs while wearing all of that equipment.

"How heavy is this?" Nathan asked, a little out of breath.

"About forty kilos," I answered. "Ready to try going up there?" I pointed to the 110-foot aerial ladder.

We got them both in harnesses and buddied up with someone from the crew. Sidney climbed to the top twice—he forgot to take a picture the first time—but Nathan made it only about a third of the way up before looking down. "Ah, I think I'm good. I'm not a huge fan of heights."

Towards the end of their visit, I went over to Sidney.

"You know, I once refereed one of your games when you were a kid. You were skating circles around guys even then."

"What a small world!" he said. "Do you still referee?"

"Not much. I do play hockey every week, though. A lot of us here do. It's our stress relief."

"What do you mean?"

I explained to Sidney what hockey meant for us and the healing role it could have for many first responders. I told him about the Ray Kline Memorial Hockey Tournament, the history of it and why we do it.

"That's amazing that your mom drops the puck at every championship game," he said.

If my dad could see the tournament and the good work it's doing within the community, he would be very happy. For my dad, hockey was all about being part of a team, working hard, and celebrating when you had the chance. He thought about firefighting the same way. "It's about being there for people when they need you," he would often say. And that's what we try to do, on and off the ice.

Pat Kline has been a firefighter with the Halifax Fire Department for over thirty years, fifteen of which as a captain, and a critical care paramedic at the QEII Health Sciences Centre Foundation. In 2013, he was awarded the Exemplary Service Medal by Nova Scotia's lieutenant governor for his service. Pat lives in Halifax.

Until the Job Is Done

Bob McKenzie

*It looks like a standard official's jersey. . . . Like Kevin
himself, it's technically still in one piece, but there's a jagged
cut, from the bottom of the front of the jersey right up to the
neckline. That jagged line is where the EMS personnel used
scissors to hastily cut it off him in order to save his life.*

If revisiting the life-altering moment that nearly killed him some
nine years earlier is disturbing to Kevin Brown, he shows no visible
signs.

The thirty-four-year-old picks up and flips open his laptop with
his right hand. He nimbly navigates the touch pad with his fingers,
cuing up a video. He's sitting on a couch in his Sebringville, Ontario,
home, the same farmhouse in which his father grew up, a well-worn,
weathered 165-year-old structure built by his father's forebears when
they first came to Canada from Ireland in the middle of the nine-
teenth century.

His left arm is folded across his lap, just in front of the computer.
If necessary, he can lift that arm, but only to shoulder height—for example, to push a door closed or turn a light switch on or off—but he
can't really use his hand or fingers in any meaningful way. His left leg,
however, works a lot better. He can walk, but he can't flex his ankle or
wiggle his toes. There's just not a lot of feeling on much of his left side.

Kevin stares intently at the computer screen from behind his wire-rimmed glasses. His dark hair is close cropped. If you look closely—it isn't blatantly obvious, but it's there—you can see the scar line running through his hair. He can and does trace it with his finger. It starts directly over his right ear, comes forward across his temple, veers left to wrap around the upper half of his forehead. It stays pretty close to his hairline, before turning backward and running from the top middle of his forehead back to his crown, where there's a bit of a soft spot because the bone never fully fused there. From the crown, it goes down a little further, then circles back to just above his ear. It's more or less the shape of an oval.

"What's your stomach like?" Brown asks.

He knows the video that he's about to play gets pretty graphic, so if anyone is squeamish about the sight of blood all over the ice—lots of blood, his own blood—well, he's better to ask up front.

"Some people were afraid that watching the video was going to bother me," Kevin says, before pressing Play. "But it didn't."

The video is of a Junior C game from Tuesday, December 29, 2009. The Woodstock Renegades are playing host to the New Hamburg Firebirds at Southwood Arena. Woodstock is wearing their home whites, New Hamburg their road navy and burgundy. Twenty-five-year-old Kevin Brown is in the black-and-white stripes, whistle in hand, working the lines, proudly wearing the Ontario Hockey Association (OHA) crest over his heart and the BROWN nameplate across his upper back.

Eight minutes into the third period, a Woodstock defenceman rushes the puck up the left side of the ice. He circles behind the New Hamburg net and swings wide back up the boards on the other side. He threads a nice seam pass to a teammate, who cuts through the slot, and quickly fires the puck past the goalie. As he's doing so, a New Hamburg player gives him two pretty good whacks with the stick, one on the arm when he's shooting and one across the back of the legs after he's scored.

Instead of celebrating the goal, the goal scorer and the defender come together below the goal line—not in the corner, not directly behind the net either, but somewhere between the two—and once the two players are right up against the boards, the gloves come off. Linesman Bruce Byers arrives first, Kevin right behind him.

The two players wrestle, pivot, and exchange punches, dancing right alongside the end boards until they are directly behind the net. Bruce and Kevin, one on each side of the altercation, shadow them as they move, looking to get in to break up the fight. The Woodstock player is now without his jersey and shoulder pads, which have been pulled off during the fight. Bruce is to the right of the two combatants; Kevin is a little to the left but more in front of them, between the fight and the goal frame, with his back to the net. Just when it looks like the two linesmen are about to get their opening to move in, the Woodstock player forcefully yanks down his opponent, who's already bent over, and they both start falling to the ice. As the New Hamburg player falls, his right skate forcefully pinwheels off the ice, arcing wildly through the air.

The heel end of the skate blade strikes Kevin directly on the right side of his neck. Kevin immediately clutches his neck and his left knee momentarily buckles but never goes fully to the ice as he stands over the two prone players. In less than two seconds, there are two large patches of bright red blood on the white ice behind the net. Kevin, still holding his neck with his hand, turns and skates quickly towards the benches, leaving behind him a trail of blood as he disappears out of the frame. It's the freakiest, never-seen-anything-like-it hockey accident ever.

"Watching the video doesn't bother me, I think, because it helped put my mind at ease," Kevin says when it finishes. "After the accident,

I had all sorts of questions. Did I do something wrong? Did I cause this to happen? Was my position wrong? The video helped answer those questions."

He's viewed only it a handful of times. The first time was to satisfy his curiosity, to find out whether he was in any way the author of his own misfortune. On a few other occasions, he showed it to some people in the hockey officiating fraternity to get their take, which reinforced that it was just plain, old-fashioned bad luck. The worst.

Tragic as Kevin's story may be, it is really about perseverance, fortitude, brotherhood, and the hard but valiant struggle to live a full life after fate throws some pretty heavy physical, mental, and emotional burdens. It also happens to be the story of a down-to-earth pig farmer, or "bacon maker" as he calls it, who has a really dry sense of humour, a self-described "smart-ass" and occasional practical joker, who may or may not answer to the name "Peckerhead."

What is he to make of all that transpired since that December day in 2009?

He pauses for a moment. "It is what it is. If I had the power to change it . . ." he says, his voice trailing off momentarily, "but I don't. I tend to be an optimistic person. I'm lucky it turned out as well as it did."

If you're familiar with southern Ontario, you know that as you travel away from Toronto on Highway 401, past Guelph to London, the big swath of land north of the highway is famous for a couple of things. Farming and hockey. Everywhere there are farmers, hockey players, teams, and arenas. And hockey officials—referees and linesmen.

Guelph, and the general vicinity around it, including Kitchener-Waterloo, has always felt like the cradle of NHL officiating. So many NHL on-ice officials—Terry Gregson; Bill McCreary; Ray Scapinello;

Bob Hodges; the Devorski family: ex-NHL ref Paul, current linesman Greg, and their late father Bill, who was an amateur officiating legend in Ontario—were from the area. There used to be high-end officiating schools based in Guelph, and a lot of the schools' graduates stayed. The city's less than an hour's drive from Toronto—NHL rules used to stipulate that an official had to live within an hour of an NHL city—and still within easy driving distance of Buffalo and Detroit. And it's a lot less expensive than living in Toronto, too.

The one-hour rule no longer exists, but that western corridor north of the 401 between Guelph and London remains a veritable spawning ground for those wearing NHL stripes. Many current NHL on-ice officials hail from the area: Garrett Rank is from Elmira, Scott Driscoll is from Seaforth, Andrew Smith is from Kitchener, Brad Kovachik is from Woodstock, Scott Cherry is from Drayton, and then there are Steve Miller, Kendrick Nicholson, and Devin Berg, all, unbelievably, from Stratford.

This should come as no surprise, because there is so much hockey being played here. There are Ontario Hockey League teams in Guelph, Kitchener, and London. There are Junior A or B teams in those bigger centres but also in Cambridge, Waterloo, Elmira, Listowel, Stratford, St. Mary's, and Strathroy, to name only a few. There are Junior C teams in Mitchell, Tavistock, Woodstock, New Hamburg, Walkerton, and many more small towns along the way. There are multiple university, college, and high school teams and leagues— lots of senior hockey, some of it organized and sanctioned, much of it just local men's leagues, and a plethora of minor hockey teams, too.

For an aspiring hockey official, there's no place in the world that offers so much opportunity to advance from level to level, so many games in such a relatively small area, almost all of it easily accessible by car. You can use the 401 or the wide network of two-lane highways or concession roads, driving by all that flat, fertile Ontario land that is home to so many farms, be they dairy, pig, cattle, poultry and eggs, sheep and goats, oilseeds and grains, or assorted crops.

Kevin Brown is very much a product of this environment. The family farm that he grew up on—with his dad, Murray, his mom, Linda, and his younger sisters, Laurie and Janice—is a 100-acre spread near Mitchell, a small town of 3,300. The Browns raise pigs on the farm that's just a 20-kilometre hop, skip, and jump on Highway 8 west from Stratford.

As farming and hockey go, you can't come up with a better historical hockey connection than Mitchell and Stratford. Both lay claim to the legend of Howie Morenz, the Montreal Canadiens' star forward who was the best and most dynamic player of his era, from the early twenties to the late thirties, and one of the NHL's all-time greats. Born in Mitchell, later a resident of Stratford, Morenz was known as the "Mitchell Meteor" or the "Stratford Streak."

"He's claimed by everyone around here," Kevin says with a laugh. "He's the Streak if you're from Stratford or the Meteor if you're from Mitchell. The Allman arena in Stratford is on Morenz Drive; that's where the Junior B team plays. I don't know any way of proving it, but I heard that Morenz was born on the farm right beside Mom and Dad's farm. I don't know if it's true."

It might as well be now. Kevin's life growing up on a farm in Howie Morenz country was what you might expect. By age four, he was riding around with his dad in the various pieces of farm equipment. By six, he was taking a more active interest, helping in the barn with chores. He played soccer and baseball in the summer, but it was house-league hockey, as a defenceman, at the Mitchell District Arena that he loved best. He eventually gave up soccer and baseball but continued to play hockey into his teens. When he was too old for house-league hockey, he tried out for a rep team, but he didn't make it.

That was okay, though, because Kevin knew his future was in farming, not hockey. As a teenager, he went on his first "harvest run," or "wheat run," in the United States. Every May, migrant farming crews, along with their heavy equipment, from all over North America flock to Texas. Wheat ripens at a rate of about thirty miles a day, so the harvesting would start in Texas and work its way north. Texas, Oklahoma, Kansas, Nebraska, South Dakota, North Dakota. Some crews go over to Wyoming and Montana. Some of the Canadian crews continue on and go right up into Saskatchewan and Alberta. Some of the American crews switch to fall crops and head home.

A couple of years after Kevin's first run, he got a job with a crew based out of Minnesota. He was seventeen, and it was really good summer employment. But he wanted to make money in the winter,

A candid photo of Kevin working in
Oklahoma during a wheat run. This was
taken the summer before his accident.

too, so he picked up refereeing. He liked hockey and had heard he could make pretty good money being a referee.

After he graduated from the Ontario Agricultural College in 2004, Kevin's routine became well established. He would finish the spring planting season at home on the family farm. Then he would head south for the wheat run—hook up with a crew in Oklahoma in mid-June and stay until he got to North Dakota around Labour Day. He would come home in September, his pockets full of US cash at a time when the Canadian dollar was weak, and start refereeing hockey games whenever and wherever he could.

When he first started officiating, he immediately got his Level 2 referee certification, which allowed him to skip doing house-league games and move directly into rep-level hockey. He did Novice and Atom games, mostly in Mitchell or nearby Monkton. The rules were you could referee any game so long as you were two years older than the players in the game. Eventually, he got to work as a linesman in a three-man officiating crew doing Bantam rep games.

"I preferred doing the lines to reffing," he says. "I thought it was simpler. Was the player onside or offside? For icing calls, was he over centre or behind centre when he shot the puck in? It was simple. There was no figuring out intent, what is or isn't a penalty. It was easier to be consistent."

Kevin really enjoyed officiating hockey games. He still had a connection to the game he loved, and it was quite profitable, too. In fact, he was turning it into lucrative winter employment, officiating 450 games one season. He was a little sour one month because he ended up with 99 games and had wanted a clean 100. He would have had it, too, but a high school game got cancelled because of snow.

He loved doing high school hockey in Kitchener because it paid upwards of $70 a game, and he'd also get mileage to drive there. Lots of officials who had day jobs couldn't do high school games, so Kevin eagerly embraced them, but he would work any game he could. Because he was bouncing around from rink to rink, town to town, he would always stop at Subway, grab a foot-long sandwich, eat half before the game, maybe finish the other half between periods or after the game. He recalled one day doing as many as seven or eight games—a morning high school game in Listowel, three high school tournament games in Waterloo at eleven, twelve, and one, then going to Stratford for another game at three. He ended the day with three minor hockey games in Mitchell at night.

Kevin also enjoyed the camaraderie, being part of the officiating brotherhood. He would often do games with his great friend Bob Skinner, a dairy farmer. They were inseparable and loved nothing more than giving each other the gears. Bob would only ever call Kevin "Peckerhead." Affectionately, of course.

Kevin would give it right back, too. There's a lot of squatting in dairy farming, and when Bob and Kevin were doing a lot of games, Bob would sometimes jokingly complain about his legs feeling old, so Kevin found a discarded walker and modified it by putting a set of old skate blades on the bottom. When Bob showed up for their next game, the walker was there for him. Kevin suspected there would one day be payback.

"The Skinners always jokingly referred to me as their third son because of how much time Bob and I spent together refereeing," Kevin says.

Officiating was fun. But in the back of Kevin's mind, he thought that if the stars all aligned, if everything worked out, maybe one day he'd be forced to have to make a tough decision between farming or going pro with officiating. He was, however, also being realistic in a way you might expect from a farmer, ever the pragmatist.

"The wheels were definitely turning on how I could progress to the next level," he says, "but, honestly, I didn't think my skating was good enough. It was probably more of a pipe dream, a long shot, however you want to phrase it. But I still thought about it."

To get to that next level, Kevin would first have to become an OHA official, which would allow him to do junior-level games that might open doors to even higher levels. In order to get noticed by the OHA, many officials would go to a summer exposure camp, the now-defunct North American School of Officiating (NASO) in Guelph, which was run by NHL officiating alumni and featured NHL on-ice officials as instructors and counsellors. But Kevin couldn't go to NASO. He was on the wheat run in the summer.

In the summer of 2008, Kevin decided to stay home. He knew this would be his big chance to attend NASO, to impress the OHA brass and finally make the grade. Unfortunately, he had a terrible showing. He wasn't in great physical condition, and his skating, as he feared, was an issue. He was deeply disappointed by his shortcomings, and when the next season rolled around, he went back to his old routine, doing minor and non-OHA senior games, to keep busy and to make money.

The next summer, NASO was no more, but the OHA had started its own summer evaluation camp. While he was still interested in finding a way to become an OHA official, he intended to go back to the United States for the harvest run. He had some people in his corner, officiating fraternity friends in the area who were lobbying on his behalf. As a result, Kevin had been assigned to work the Ontario Hockey Federation Juvenile AAA championship in Ajax. He was told the OHA would use his work at that tournament as a test.

He failed. Again. It was the same story as at NASO—his skating. He took off for the harvest run that summer, not expecting to hear any good news from the OHA. It was over and done with, as far as he was concerned.

If Kevin had lost hope, his good friend and fellow ref Chris Faulkner had not. Chris was doing some supervisory work for the OHA, and that summer he continued to push the OHA to give Kevin a chance.

Kevin was in South Dakota—nineteen hours and more than two thousand kilometres from home—the night before he was leaving to head north. He surprisingly had some Wi-Fi, so he jumped on and checked his email. There was a message telling him that things didn't look too good.

Well, at least I know where things are at, he thought.

The next day, he was about to head out on the road when his phone rang. It was the OHA supervisor. *Why's he calling me?*

The supervisor was phoning to ask Kevin if he was interested in officiating OHA games. Twelve hours earlier his chances were seemingly dead in the water, and now the supervisor was offering him an opportunity to officiate. When he got off the phone, he had a text from Chris. All it said was, "You owe me huge."

"To this day, I still blame him for getting me in this condition I'm in," Kevin says. Then he starts laughing, because, of course, it's a joke. A pretty good one, too. Kevin lost a lot of things because of his accident. His sense of humour wasn't one of them.

The last day of the life Kevin had always known was pretty typical, which meant it was busy. The 2009–10 season was his first as an OHA linesman, and he was taking full advantage, getting fifty bucks a game to work as a linesman at Junior C games all over the area, though he realized he was going to have start scaling back his officiating. He was getting busier with "real" work.

He'd moved out of his parents' house in Mitchell into the original family farmhouse in Sebringville, and within the previous year, Kevin had gotten a contract to look after some pigs. He also had an actual nine-to-five job, working at the parts counter of Stratford Farm Equipment, on top of his heavy officiating schedule. Eventually, he wanted to do just one junior and one senior game on the weekend, but for now, he was making it work.

Just before Christmas, he was lining an OHA junior game in Thamesford, and his lining partner that night, who was from Windsor but going to school in London, asked Kevin for a favour. Could Kevin work a Junior C game in Woodstock for him on December 29? He planned on being home for the holidays.

"No problem," Kevin said.

He was scheduled to work recreational hockey that same night in nearby Monkton, but he easily found someone to take his rec job. It would be more challenging to do the Junior C game, and he wanted to do higher-calibre games to try to advance up the ladder. It would be a busy couple of days—Stratford had a Silver Stick qualifier between Christmas and New Year's, and Kevin was booked to work the Midget final the day after the Junior C Woodstock game.

On December 29, 2009, Kevin's alarm went off at four thirty a.m. He was in the barn, checking on the pigs, by five. He did an hour or so of chores, then returned to the house, where he showered, had breakfast, and prepared for the long day ahead. He had to be in Woodstock by six thirty p.m. for the seven thirty game, and he would have to leave straight from work at Stratford Farm, so Kevin packed his skates, his officiating gear, a suit, a tie, and his contact lenses—he wanted to look the part of an OHA official—in his Ford F-150 truck and set off for the day.

After he was done at Stratford Farm, he stopped at the Subway shop to grab a sandwich, then drove forty kilometres to the Southwood Arena in Woodstock, where he met the rest of the

London-based officiating crew in the parking lot. They headed inside to get ready for the game.

Before he stepped out on the ice, there was just one more thing to make sure of. The same thing he did before every game he officiated. It was his only real superstition.

"I always made sure to put my right skate on first," he says, "the theory being I always wanted to get off on the right foot."

After that, Kevin remembers just bits of the last game he ever officiated.

"There was a problem with the clock, early on in the game," he recalls. "The buzzer kept going off. I guess there must have been a house-league game before the Junior C game because the buzzer was going off every two or three minutes. They had to fix that."

It wasn't a particularly rough game. Woodstock tied the game, 4–4, with 11:22 left in the third period. That's when the postgoal shenanigans between the Woodstock player and the New Hamburg player started below the goal line. Fights happen. Kevin was there to break them up. It was part of his job, and there was no reason to believe this one would be any different.

The refs are taught to intervene once the players are on the ice, to get their arms around them and interlock their hands and fingers and wrap them up so they can't swing at each other.

"I was going down to my knees for a bear hug when I felt liquid running down the right side of my body, but I wasn't sure what it was or where it was coming from. *If it's on my right side, it could be blood,* I thought. *If it's blood, it's probably coming from my neck. It could be fairly major with arteries and veins there. I better not spend too much time here.*

Kevin has that farm-boy mentality that says to keep going until the job is done, and his job was to separate the fighters, but he knew

*This photo captures the moment right
before Kevin's life changed forever.*

if he kept trying to do that, it might not be good for him, so he peeled out of there. That liquid he felt, of course, was his own blood. The carotid artery, which carries blood from the heart to the brain, head, and face, had been severed by the skate blade. Kevin's heart was still pumping the blood, but it was going all over the ice instead of to his brain.

Kevin realized he was in distress, but there are two versions of what happened next: what actually happened, and what Kevin, retrospectively, thought might have happened or what he would have liked to have happened.

"I thought I made it to the players' bench on my own," he says. "But other stories I've seen or heard since then said I didn't make it that far. I don't remember being pulled through the players' bench door. The next thing I remember, I was on the bench. I guess some-one put me there. There were a bunch of people around, putting pressure on my neck with towels. They were asking me, 'Who should we call?'"

Multiple 911 calls were being made by those in attendance at Southwood Arena. Cory Smith, a reporter then for the *Woodstock Sentinel-Review*, was there, covering the game. Later, for the *Stratford Beacon Herald*, he described what happened that night. "It's an image that's etched into my memory. Blood spurted from Kevin's neck like a scene from a horror movie as he tried to clasp his hand over the wound. There was a gasp, almost in unison, from hundreds of spectators in the arena as they realized the possibility of someone dying on the ice."

Smith said the training staffs for both New Hamburg and Wood-stock, led by New Hamburg's trainer Greg Henning, who was also a medic in the Canadian Armed Forces reserve, attended to Kevin. They talked to him, trying to keep him conscious, and applied pres-sure with towels to prevent him from bleeding out. A nurse in the crowd, Paula Thomson, rushed down to help out. They were doing everything they could to save a life.

Kevin recalls being thirsty, asking for a drink of water, but Paula, the nurse, said that wasn't a good idea. She had taken charge of the situation and had likely known that Kevin was going to need surgery.

Obviously, Kevin was in shock. On one level, he knew he was badly injured. On another, though, he was thinking in more conven-tional, practical terms.

"All I was thinking was that I was scheduled to work the Midget final in Stratford the next night," Kevin says. "I thought I'd go to hos-pital, get stitched up, and still be able to do the game the next night. I obviously didn't know how bad I was. I started to think about the officiating assigner in Stratford, how he's a good guy and means well, but could get pretty hot and bothered if people cancel on him at the last minute, especially in a tournament where there are daytime games. Chappy, one of the players on New Hamburg, also did some refereeing in Stratford, so when they asked me who they should call, I told them, 'I want to talk to Chappy. Go get Chappy.' He would be able to tell the assigner that I was a question mark for my assignment the next day. Of course, no one knew who the hell Chappy was. I was trying to remember what number he was wearing and when I finally figured it out, they brought him over. As soon as I told him to make the call, I felt better."

Beyond that, it's mostly all a blur or nothing at all.

"I sort of remember the ambulance being there, I think it drove on the ice," Kevin says. "I feel like I had a flashback to *Happy Gilmore*, where the doctor tells Happy he shouldn't be playing after he's been hit by a car and Happy decides he's going to carry on anyway. In my mind, I said to myself, 'Oh, good, the ambulance is here. I'm going to stand up and walk over to it.' I don't think that happened— I may have dreamt it—but that's what I wanted to do. Once I was in the ambulance, I remember I just had one thought: 'I hope this isn't how my career ends, leaving the ice in an ambulance.'"

For as much bad luck as Kevin had that night, there was some serendipity, too. Southwood Arena is less than a kilometre from the Woodstock General Hospital. The EMS crew received the emergency call to go to the arena at 9:22 p.m. A minute later, they were mobile. The ambulance arrived at the arena at 9:26, and within two minutes, the EMS personnel were working on Kevin. They reported that Kevin was conscious and alert, but very pale, cool, and diaphoretic. By 9:39, the ambulance had returned to the hospital and the EMS team had officially handed over responsibility for Kevin to emergency room staff.

An emergency room doctor estimated Kevin had probably lost a full litre of blood already. He was intubated, started on a blood transfusion with as many as six units of blood, and prepared for lifesaving surgery. At 9:55, he was in the operating room. If this had happened to him at a game in Listowel, where the nearest hospital was over fifty kilometres away, he likely would never have made it.

In the operating room, the doctor couldn't immediately find any blood pressure and Kevin's pulse was 153—more than double the average resting rate. The doctor surgically repaired Kevin's severed carotid artery, but his blood pressure was still low, and he was concerned that Kevin might suffer a large stroke. After Kevin was out of surgery, he was transferred to London's Victoria Hospital to see a vascular surgeon there.

Meanwhile, medical personnel were trying to locate his family. His sister Janice was able to make it to the hospital in Woodstock to see Kevin before he was sent to London, but his sister Laurie just missed him. The hospital eventually reached his parents, who were in Haliburton on a dog-sledding outing, and they immediately began the four-hour drive to meet Kevin in London, where both his sisters were waiting.

At some point, the Woodstock doctor's worst fears were realized. Kevin says that he isn't even sure exactly when, but he did indeed suffer a "significant right hemispheric stroke," which negatively affected his mobility and feeling on the left side of his body. It would get worse.

While in hospital in London, Kevin experienced significant swelling in his brain. So on New Year's Eve, the doctors performed what's medically known as a "right decompressive hemicraniotomy." In other words, they removed a big piece of his skull so that his swollen brain would not be constricted. The piece of bone, the so-called flap that doctors removed, was stored in a "bone bank," to be reattached some months later, when the swelling went down. Kevin was then put into a medically induced coma for a week.

"I have flashes of memories from when I first arrived at the hospital in Woodstock, but it's mostly a whole bunch of nothing for quite some time, just a black hole," he says. "The next thing I remember is waking up in the London hospital with a lot of people around me. I was hooked up to all sorts of wires, I couldn't talk because of the tubes down my throat, and I was told I missed New Year's and that Canada had lost to the United States in the 2010 World Junior Hockey Championship."

Kevin didn't have a clue what had happened to him, and he was bombarded with information when he awoke.

"Don Cherry mentioned you on *Coach's Corner*."

"The barn is fine, things are looked after."

While those thoughts were comforting to him, more pressing was the realization that his left arm and leg didn't move. He was also in and out of pain.

As he slowly began to comprehend what had happened, his family tried their best to keep up his spirits. One of his sisters acknowledged all the tubes and wires, the IV lines, and said: "We'll get you hooked up to a beer keg."

Kevin thought that was funny. If he was to be there for a while, he'd have to maintain a sense of humour. It would be too boring and dull if he didn't.

On one occasion, he couldn't locate his call button to get the nurse, so he freelanced a little. *I'll just get out of bed and go find the nurse*, he thought. He hadn't walked in two weeks and had half a skull, so he threw some pillows on the floor in case he fell. Sure enough, he went down. He couldn't even crawl. He grabbed a pillow and lay on the floor until the nurses came to do rounds and found him.

He laughs at the memory now. Even funnier was the realization that if he needed a nurse to come in, all he had to do was disconnect the lead wire of his heart monitor and wait.

"You rocket up the nurse's priority list if they think you have flat-lined," he says. "Rather quickly, too."

The old Kevin—the prankster and wise guy—was still very much there inside the new but not necessarily improved Kevin. In the immediate days after coming out of the coma, Kevin used hand signals to try to communicate with his mom and dad. He also had a small tablet he could write on. He used his good hand, his right hand, to mimic driving with a steering wheel.

His dad caught on right away. "Do you mean autosteer?" he asked.

Kevin nodded, gave the thumbs-up.

Before the accident, Kevin had ordered a new tractor for the farm. There's a feature or option called autosteer that allows the driver to use GPS satellite navigation to steer the tractor. If you plug in the coordinates and chart what's called an A–B line, the GPS basically makes the tractor drive itself on the prescribed course. Kevin was effectively telling his dad to make sure the new tractor was equipped with autosteer because he didn't figure to be nimble enough to steer it himself. This was a good sign. Kevin was already starting to think of life after the hospital, demonstrating that he wasn't going to let this stroke and his physical limitations stop him from working his farm.

When Kevin's mom and dad decided he was strong enough to have visitors outside of immediate family, Bob Skinner and his wife were the first to stop by. That was a given.

Kevin still couldn't talk, and as soon as the Skinners arrived, he started trying to pull back the bedcovers and get his functional right hand under his hospital gown and pull it back, too. No one understood what he was trying to do.

"Mom was freaking out," Kevin says. "She thought that I'd completely lost my mind."

Fifteen minutes after the Skinners left, Bob called Kevin's mom. "Ask Kevin if he was trying to call me Peckerhead."

She repeated the question to Kevin. When he gave her a thumbs-up, she realized that he had been trying to make a joke.

"When I saw Bob come into my room, I wanted to make sure he knew that I wasn't so sick that I couldn't give the gears to him," Kevin says now, laughing as he reminisces. "Bob later said that once he knew I was trying to call him Peckerhead he knew that I was going to be okay."

If the incident was indicative of anything, it was that Kevin had not lost his sense of humour. It was a clear sign to family and friends that Kevin was still himself.

Kevin was on the long, hard road to recovery. Just a week after coming out of the coma, he was admitted to the Parkwood Institute, a London rehabilitation facility that helps stroke victims and those with spinal cord injuries prepare and adapt for their lives ahead. No sooner was he there than there was an effort to get him out on a day pass.

On January 30, 2010, the community of Stratford was the primary host of the tenth anniversary of *Hockey Day in Canada*, the annual daylong celebration of Canadiana that is broadcast for more than twelve hours on *Hockey Night in Canada*. The hometown Junior B Cullitons were playing host to the St. Marys Lincolns at the Allman that day. *Hockey Night's* Ron MacLean and Don Cherry would be there, and Don and Tim Taylor, a Stratford native and former NHL player, were scheduled to drop the puck.

As part of the festivities, Steve Miller, a NHL linesman and Stratford native, had organized a training clinic for house-league referees. Kevin, who was vice president of the local referees' association at the time, was originally supposed to be helping out at the clinic, but that, of course, was no longer possible. The organizers still wanted to include and honour Kevin on *Hockey Day in Canada*, so they called up his parents. If Kevin could get to Stratford, they would bump Don Cherry and Tim Taylor from opening face-off duties at the Cullitons game and let Kevin do it.

Kevin had been in Parkwood for only eight days, and naturally, the doctors were a bit reluctant to let him out for the day, but they consented under the condition that he was accompanied by a nurse. Paula Thomson, the same nurse who'd helped save his life, agreed to do it. The other stipulation was that Kevin had to wear a helmet, which would be a fixture any time he was on his feet until his bone flap was finally reattached in late May, a month after he was released from Parkwood permanently.

The fact that he preempted Grapes and Stanley Cup champ Taylor from the ceremonial puck drop and got some *Hockey Day in Canada* and *Hockey Night in Canada* face time and national recognition amuses Kevin even now. The framed picture of him wearing a

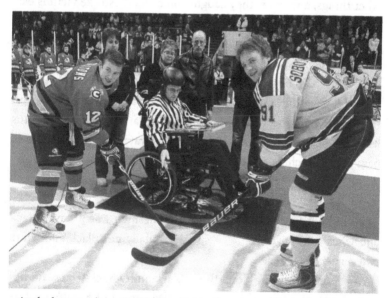

As the honoured guest of Hockey Day in Canada, *Kevin dropped the puck for the Junior B game at the Allman Arena in Stratford. Behind him, from left to right, are Paula Thomson, his mom, Linda, and his dad, Murray.*

referee's jersey and helmet, sitting in a wheelchair to drop the puck, is on display in his farmhouse, but he's the first to tell you that he doesn't remember everything that happened that day. It's all still a bit of a blur.

After *Hockey Day in Canada*, news of Kevin's injury had spread, and the community at large had rallied around him, sending thoughts and good wishes, raising a total of $40,000 to help with his treatments.

Back at Parkwood, Kevin continued to work on his mobility and functionality. His spirits were generally good. He jokingly formed a patients' union with other stroke and spinal cord injury victims there, ostensibly to have a few laughs. He liked to rib the nursing staff. They would lecture the patients on good nutrition, among other things, and once, they caught some elderly stroke victims eating small bags of potato chips from out of a vending machine in the patient lounge. Kevin decided to have a little fun, and when he was out on a day pass, he stopped at a grocery store and came back with family-size bags of chips and dip for those same patients. He caught an earful from the staff for that one, but he had a good rapport with them, and when he was discharged from Parkwood three months later, the nursing staff gave him a going-away present. A couple of bags of potato chips. No dip, though.

The old hockey slogan about refs and linesmen was always "Black and white and never right." It should actually be "Black and white and very tight."

As soon as anyone dons those black-and-white stripes, he becomes part of a fraternal order. As word spread of Kevin's misfortune, the support from the hockey officiating community was strong and immediate.

"I was blown out of the water by it," Kevin says. "It really brought to light and reinforced how small the hockey world is and how strong the officiating brotherhood is. I got a hat from a referee in Japan. I got all sorts of emails wishing me well from all corners of the hockey world."

One of those emails was from Dave Jackson, a veteran NHL ref who himself was on the sidelines because of a major knee injury at the time of Kevin's accident. He wrote that he had been feeling a bit sorry for himself, and Kevin's accident had given him some much-needed perspective. He was very supportive and had some kind words for him.

Terry Gregson sent flowers. Greg Devorski sent an autographed picture of himself and Wayne Gretzky from an NHL game. There was an autographed jersey from Don Koharski and an NHL ref's shirt signed by all the NHL officials, as well as multiple other framed photos, mementos, and visible signs of support.

Perhaps his most treasured officiating possession is the striped jersey he was wearing in his last game in Woodstock. It looks like a standard official's jersey—black and white stripes, OHA logo on the upper-left chest area, Hockey Canada logo on one arm, Canadian flag and Ontario Hockey Federation (OHF) logo on the other arm, and the BROWN nameplate across the upper back. But Kevin's jersey is different. Like Kevin himself, it's technically still in one piece, but there's a jagged cut, from the bottom of the front of the jersey right up to the neckline. That jagged line is where the EMS personnel used scissors to hastily cut it off him in order to save his life.

The jersey's been washed thoroughly, but if you look closely, there's a slight red tinge to the embroidered Hockey Canada logo on the right arm. That, of course, is the residue of Kevin's blood, although it's really quite something that there's virtually no other evidence of blood anywhere else on the shirt. That jersey, jagged cut line and all, means so much to Kevin. No words can do that bond justice, which is why Kevin has effectively replicated his official's jersey on his body. In March 2017, he got the black-and-red hockey puck OHA logo tattooed on the left side of his chest, right where it would be if he were wearing his striped jersey. Exactly a year later, he got the full-size rectangular black nameplate with white lettering right across his upper back, precisely where it would be if the jersey were on his back. The tattoos are meant to be motivation, but also a memorial.

"They make me feel like I'm part of something," he says.

A freak accident took so much away from Kevin Brown, but the OHA logo—the elusive one he chased for so many years—and that nameplate across his back serve as his lifelong reminder. Once an on-ice official, always an on-ice official—then, now, and forever more.

Since leaving the hospital in 2010, Kevin's had good days, bad days, and everything in between, but he's not one to complain, and he's made noteworthy strides. About one-third of his brain was significantly damaged by the stroke, but thanks in large part to Parkwood and the associated Community Stroke Rehabilitation Team, an outreach program with specialists who visit stroke victims right in their rural homes, Kevin learned how to walk again. The larger muscle mass in his left leg responded to state-of-the-art treatment much better than the smaller muscles of his left arm and hand did, but he continues to go to the gym and physiotherapy twice a week in Stratford.

And he's turned them into social outings as well. He jokingly refers to Rachel, the kinesiologist he works with, as his "minion." Kevin pushes her buttons for a laugh and enjoys the camaraderie that comes from their banter.

"She abuses me with exercise," he says. "I abuse her with smart-ass comments. She's a really good sport."

His physical improvements, however, have hit a wall, but he keeps up his physical routine so he has the muscle mass in case there's ever new stroke-recovery technology. It can be a grind, though. Fatigue is often a companion and can hinder his decision-making ability. According to Kevin, it takes longer for him to think through problems, and he doesn't process information as quickly as he used to.

While Kevin has the obvious physical scars of his ordeal, notably the one that meanders around his skull, the things he's experienced have dented him in other ways. After he left the hospital, the Woodstock surgeon who repaired his carotid artery and saved his life told him if the skate puncture wound had been an inch further back, he would have been paralyzed. If the full skate blade had sliced his neck and jugular vein, he would have died on the ice.

"Hearing that was hard," Kevin says. "It was probably one of the most sickening moments I had."

In the wake of Kevin's accident, OHA on-ice officials were mandated to wear neck protectors.

Another tough day was when he was still in Parkwood and the doctor told him he would never have fine finger movement on his left hand. For Kevin, a farmer who needed his fingers to do mechanical work, that news was a bombshell. He was still full of defiance and resolve, though he would get worn down on that front.

For a time, Kevin was determined he would skate again. He had a brace attached to his left skate boot and rigged it up to give himself a fighting chance, but he didn't realize how much ankle movement is required for skating. His balance wasn't great to begin with, and the stroke has left him with foot drop, which means if his foot isn't supported, it just drops. The more he tried, the more he was reminded of how much he'd lost physically and how much he'd gone backwards.

———

"At the start, I was probably naive, too full of optimism. I always used the Frosty the Snowman line in the hospital, 'I'll be back someday.' But I was being naive and overly optimistic. Reality set in."

So, quite frankly, did depression. For a time, he took medication to combat it, but he didn't think the meds worked particularly well. There's a particular program that really assists him in dealing with his depression, and he goes back there for a "top-up" every few years. In general, he prefers a more holistic approach.

"What works the best for me is to keep busy," he says. "I went from one hundred miles per hour—reffing, farming, working a job, always on the go—and I have to reinvent myself. I have to find ways to keep busy and occupied. The busier I am, the better. If I have too much time to sit around, that isn't good for me."

He takes his victories when and where he can find them. In 2014, he got his driver's license back for the first time since his accident. That was a game changer. He needs a steering wheel apparatus—a spinner knob—and a couple of other minor modifications in order to drive his F-150 pickup truck one handed, but being mobile gave him back a large measure of independence.

He's still living on his own at the farmhouse—outside of when his dad briefly stayed with him on weekends after he was discharged from hospital in 2010. He knows help is there if he needs it but likes the idea of bearing down to overcome his obstacles, being his own man.

He doesn't expect any special treatment, and he didn't get any either. When he arrived home to the farm after being discharged from Parkwood, that old walker he rigged up to poke fun at Bob Skinner was sitting right there at the farmhouse door.

"I had a feeling when I gave that walker to Bob I would be seeing it again one day," Kevin says, laughing.

Kevin doesn't think about the "what-ifs." He's more of a get-it-done type of guy, one who would rather be productive than think about what could have been. Instead, he carries on and makes the best of his situation.

He's a farmer, after all. He's doing cash crop and custom work. People with farmland who may not have the machinery or time to cost-efficiently tend to their own crops hire Kevin to do it for them, using his equipment and sweat equity. He does his own bookwork, and if it's planting or harvesting season, he's out in the fields working because people depend on him. From mid-April to June, it's busy. The wheat harvest starts in July, drags into August. The fall, from mid to late September and right into November, is busy. He gets help if he needs it, but once the fields are set up, he can run the equipment.

"It's just pushing buttons, which I'm fairly good at," Kevin says, smiling. "I just sit in the tractor and run it on autosteer. Push those buttons."

It is, as the saying goes, a living.

Kevin, by nature, focuses far less on what was taken from him and far more on what he's been given, which is to say he's big on gratitude and expressing it to those who have been good to him. In December 2010, almost on the first anniversary of his accident, Kevin hosted a dinner at the Boston Pizza in Stratford for the many people who did something to help him out in his time of need, including Paula Thomson and Greg Henning. Seven years later, he took his dad, Paula, Greg, plus the referee Mike Logan and linesman Bruce Byers, who were on the ice in Woodstock with him, to the Canada-USA game of the 2017 World Junior Championship at the Air Canada Centre in Toronto.

"They had to witness all of what happened to me," Kevin says. "I didn't want them to be forgotten."

And Kevin paid back Chris Faulkner, the friend who got him in "this condition" by hooking him up with the OHA, by taking him to the 2012 World Junior Championship bronze- and gold-medal games in Buffalo.

Kevin's officiating days are over, of course, but that doesn't mean he can't help out with the local Stratford Referees Association, scheduling and assigning referees for the house league and doing some mentoring work with young officials. After all the support he received from his community, he wants to give back any way he can. He's not sure how, but he knows he has more to give—perhaps with the Heart and Stroke Foundation or a charity golf tournament for stroke and spinal cord injuries.

In the meantime, Kevin will do what he's been doing. Living his best life, one day at a time, and when he spends time reflecting, he won't ask, "Why me?" He'll ask, "How can I help others?" Because at the end of the day, Kevin doesn't see himself as any kind of hero.

"I don't think I've done anything extraordinary or exceptional," he says. "I was twenty-five years old when my life changed, and the way I look at it, I've got forty-five to fifty years to go. That's a long time to be walking around feeling sorry for myself and not doing anything with my life, and I don't want to live like that. I was thrown into a situation, and I didn't have a choice or time to debate the outcome. I'm dealing with what I have to, as anyone else would.

"Paula Thomson, Greg Henning, the other Woodstock and New Hamburg trainers, the EMS people, the doctors, the nurses who helped me—they are more heroic than me. They're the real heroes."

Kevin Brown is a farmer in Sebringville, Ontario, and a former Ontario Hockey Association on-ice official. In 2009, he suffered a stroke as a result of an on-ice injury. When he's not working in the fields, he continues his rehabilitation by working out and doing physiotherapy in nearby Stratford and mentors young hockey officials.

Afterword

Bob McKenzie

It's one thing to know something, quite another to actually see and feel it. Case in point: my involvement with *Everyday Hockey Heroes*. I *knew* from the moment I became associated with the book, which was published in October 2018, that it would be inspirational. The stories were simply too good for that not to happen. But I must admit, even I was taken aback at the emotional impact the book had on so many, including me.

Especially me.

At our last book signing before Christmas in downtown Toronto, Jim Lang and I were joined by Wayne St. Denis, Christian Holmes, and Brock McGillis. It was my first opportunity to meet and talk to them. I also got to meet some of their friends and family, all of whom were so proud and excited. I had already read Wayne, Christian, and Brock's stories; I already knew how inspiring they were, but to witness how thrilled and humbled they were to be part of this book, to get to know them a bit personally, well, it was moving on a level that is hard to put into words.

It was much the same a couple weeks earlier when Jim and I were joined by Ben Fanelli and Kevin Brown at another book signing at Kitchener Memorial Auditorium during an OHL Rangers game. I had already known the special bond Ben shared with Kitchener

Rangers fans, many of whom were in the building the night Ben suffered a traumatic brain injury on the ice. That bond was why I knew Ben's story had to be in the book. To actually see and feel that connection between Ben and the Rangers fans, though, was amazing. Throughout the evening, so many people stopped by to see Ben, to say hi, to ask how he was doing, and to tell him they remembered the day he was injured and the day he returned to the ice. I could tell how much their warmth and care meant to Ben. It was so tangible, so palpable. It was infectious.

Since I wrote Kevin Brown's story, I already knew how much it meant to both him and me to be able to share his journey, but again, to be able to meet Kevin's family and those who were instrumental in saving his life, to see how moved Kevin was to be part of it all . . . I'm not sure I was fully prepared for how it made me feel.

After publication, there were so many of these moments where I felt like being a part of this book was some sort of transcendent experience. Two other moments stand out.

The first was at a book signing at Costco in Ajax, Ontario. Among the many who came out to get a book signed that day were two women who arrived together and asked me to sign their books for their hockey-playing sons. One of the women told me how much her son loves hockey and would look forward to reading the stories in the book. The other woman noted that her son had been in an automobile accident some number of months earlier but he, too, loved hockey so much. I told her I was sorry to hear about the accident and hoped her son was okay. She paused and softly said he had died in the accident.

It was so heartbreaking, but it was also such a tender, loving moment as she asked me to sign the book for her late son and told me how much he would have enjoyed reading it. Whenever I pick up the book now, I think of that woman and I hope that maybe some of the stories in these pages have given her a fleeting moment of comfort amid what has to be such a terrible loss.

The other *Everyday Hockey Heroes* moment I won't soon forget was a book signing at the West Edmonton Mall. There was a large group of people there to get their books signed, and as I was doing that, I noticed a young woman with a baby in a stroller, standing off to the side and talking at length with Catherine Whiteside, Simon & Schuster's publicity manager. As the crowd thinned, Catherine introduced me to the young woman, who had recently immigrated to Canada. In broken English, she told Catherine that she wanted the book made out to her baby boy, who had been born in Canada. I signed the book and we took a photo together.

The woman knew nothing about hockey other than how much the game means to Canadians, and it was so very important to her that her son grow up to love this game, too. It reminded me of Karina Potvin's heartwarming story about Mohammed, Ahmad, and Ismael, the young Syrian boys desperate to learn the game. And it was another incredibly touching moment between a loving mother and her son. I was so humbled to be some small part of it, and I still smile when I think of that little boy growing up and one day reading this book of stories because his dear mother was so intent on making sure he felt at home here in Canada.

I know I'm not the only one who has been emotionally affected by this book. In the next few pages, you'll hear from Craig Cunningham about the incredible things he's been up to since the book published, and from Kevin Brown, Ben Fanelli, Brock McGillis, and others on how the book has impacted them.

As for me, I knew from the outset this project was something special. But to actually *see* and *feel* how it brought people together, over and over, has been a remarkable experience. I knew the book would celebrate hockey and those connected to the sport by their love of the game. What I didn't realize is how intensely those feelings would go beyond the book and even beyond hockey.

Craig Cunningham

Since I got hurt and lost my leg, I have been on the ice around eight to ten times. I would wear a regular skate boot on my prosthetic leg, but it was difficult because the skate was deadweight on the end of my leg. It's just an extra pound or so, which doesn't sound like a lot, but it makes a big difference when you have a prosthetic leg. So, when I heard that some people were skating on prosthetic legs with just the skate blade attached to the end, I was excited. *How would it feel?* I wondered. As I researched, I realized that a lot of people have found great success with this adapted prosthetic.

I contacted Peter Harsch Prosthetics to find out if I could get something similar. I connected with a prosthetist named Randell Leoncio, who is a fellow above-knee amputee, and he was able to attach the TUUK blade to the end of my leg. All that was left to do was to test it out. I called up Dallas Eakins, the head coach of the San Diego Gulls, and asked if I could practice on their rink. On April 3, 2019, I did just that.

The first time that I stepped out on the ice with the TUUK blade, I was a little freaked-out. *Holy shit*, I thought, *I can barely move!* I couldn't push off like I was used to, but the good news was that that deadweight was gone. After a few laps around the rink, I got a sense of how the ankle moved with the skate at the bottom of the prosthetic and began to feel more comfortable. I had given my leg time to heal and now I was skating again. It felt like coming home.

Since my injury, I've gotten back into the hockey world in a different way, scouting for the Arizona Coyotes, which I enjoy. But in the back of my mind, I kept thinking about getting into coaching and player development. I have been through all the ups and downs of pro hockey. I spent time in the minors and got called up, only to play four minutes, so I understand the mental struggles that come with being a fringe player in the NHL, and I know I can help other players by talking about my experiences. Coaching is my next goal for my hockey career, but that means being able to skate on the ice, and I was not sure that I would be able to do that. After skating with the TUUK blade, I am confident that I will get to the point where I skate well enough to coach and mentor other players. I won't have any more physical limitations and I'll be able to make decisions about my career based on what I want to do, not just settling for what I'm capable of doing.

I had asked Randell to film me that day on the ice. I posted the video online, mainly to say thank you to Dallas Eakins and the San Diego Gulls for letting me use their practice rink. I'm not a part of their organization, and they could have easily said no, but Dallas is a great guy. I was most excited to send the video to Ray Ferraro. He's a man who has mentored me for years and has done so much for me and my family. I also sent it to the staff with the Tucson Roadrunners and the Arizona Coyotes to show them how well I am doing and to let them know I'm able to undertake other hockey roles within the organization.

After I posted the video, I didn't look at my phone for around an hour. When I finally did, I must have had more than fifty or sixty text messages from different people who had seen it. In less than twenty-four hours, it received more than a hundred thousand views. That freaked me out a bit, but the response was amazing.

One thing I have learned about the hockey world is that we are all so competitive when we play against each other. Off the ice, it is a different story. From the day that I collapsed on the ice until today, past players, coaches, and managers I've played with or known have reached out to me and offered their support. That is what makes hockey so special: the bond of brothers on your team and across the entire sport.

I am almost back. I am not coming back to play, but I want to get to the point where I feel at home every time I step out on the ice.

Kevin Brown

When I was seventeen, I started refereeing as a part-time job, a hobby, because I love the game of hockey. That love didn't die when I was injured on the ice, but my life has been a bit of a roller coaster since. It's been ten years since my injury, and as Bob wrote in my story, I still have good days, bad days, and everything in between, but last year was particularly tough for me, both personally and professionally.

In early 2018, I was questioning the direction of my life and wondering where I was headed. Then Bob contacted me and asked about telling my story in a book called *Everyday Hockey Heroes*. I was unsure of what to expect and how things would go, but Bob promised he would do right by me, so I said yes.

At one point last year, I was in therapy and feeling particularly low. Then my therapist said, "You've got this book and a couple other things on the go. You can't throw those things away." In truth, the publication of *Everyday Hockey Heroes* was one of the bright spots that pulled me through. And Bob kept his word. He and everyone at Simon & Schuster followed through on what they said, which seems to be increasingly rare these days.

Everyday Hockey Heroes captures the spirit of hockey and everything it entails: dedication, teamwork, battling through adversity, and perseverance. I was inspired by the people in these pages who, like me, have faced injury and hardship and come out on the other side. I feel so fortunate to be a part of this book and I can honestly say it was life-changing for me. When I started refereeing, I was just trying to see how far I could take it, and when I look back on the last ten years, I feel so fortunate that hockey has given me incredible opportunities like this one. The whole experience of sharing my story and connecting with others like Ben Fanelli has encouraged me to be more open and positive. This journey has also helped me get through those bad days, and I hope they're behind me.

Ben Fanelli

This book is bigger than sport because it clearly exemplifies two things. One: people are incredibly resilient. Two: people are even more resilient when they have a sporting community around them. I am so humbled that my story is mentioned in this book. The only thing missing is the name of every selfless person who supported me when they had no idea who I was. That would fill up a whole second volume!

Christian Holmes

I never really thought that my personal journey would make its way into a book, so it was an eye-opening experience for my family and me. I didn't realize how big of an effect my life story would have on readers, but when the book was published, I received an outpouring of kind words and support that have been so uplifting. I've always dreamed of being a sportscaster, but even when I started studying journalism in college, I wasn't sure that I would be able to make it in the sports media world due to my disability. After reading the other stories in this book and hearing all these incredible tales of triumph, my thought process has changed. I'm forever grateful to be included in such an amazing book alongside amazing people.

Andi Petrillo

I felt honoured to be a part of *Everyday Hockey Heroes*, but when I saw the book and I realized the company I was in, I was overcome with gratitude. This book is proof that there are many ways to love the game of hockey and many paths to take to grow that love. And while our journeys are all different, in the end the love is equal.

Brock McGillis

I shared my story in this book because I want to break down barriers within hockey culture. My story is just one of several, but together we are all changing the game. Last fall, I had the privilege of meeting a few of the inspirational people featured in this collection, and what I saw was a number of individuals who don't fit the "hockey mold" and yet are utilizing the game to impact and evolve, not just the sport, but society as well. Their stories motivate me on a daily basis to push forward, shift culture, and strive towards equality.

Acknowledgements

Bob McKenzie

If you want to know the cold, hard truth, I don't actually like writing books, which I feel I'm allowed to say since I've written two of them. This is, I guess, No. 3.

I kind of hate it. Love the finished product; hate the process. Writing is hard. It takes a lot of words to fill a book and I agonize over too many of them. So when my pesky (but very good) book agent Brian Wood once again called to say he had a proposal for me, I did what I usually do and told him I'm not interested. He eventually managed to convey to me that Kevin Hanson of Simon and Schuster Canada had a unique proposal where I actually wouldn't have to write it all myself. Well, now, he most certainly had my attention. So thanks to Brian for being Brian; thanks to Kevin and Simon and Schuster Canada for thinking of me and introducing me to *Everyday Hockey Heroes*, but more importantly to editor Sarah St. Pierre and author Jim Lang.

They are my Dynamic Duo, my Dream Team. This is Sarah's and Jim's book more than it is mine because they did the lion's share of the real work. Outside of the foreword and the final chapter on Kevin Brown, which were my only written contributions, Jim interviewed every person profiled in *Everyday Hockey Heroes*, transcribed all those interviews and, in concert with the subjects, wrote incredible and inspiring first-person stories. I've known Jim a long time in Toronto media circles. He's a good man, a good friend, and a good writer, and he did yeoman's work on this book. As for Sarah, with apologies to the TSN Quizmaster, who in a previous life with me at the *Hockey News*, fancied himself a superstar editor, I'm afraid he has more than met his match. Sarah is the glue that binds this book. It is very much her vision. No Sarah; no book. She's smart, conscientious, driven, detailed, and committed, which is to say she was often a royal pain in my butt, like any good editor should be.

It was also Jim and Sarah who introduced me to the real heroes, the diverse group of individuals who agreed to tell their inspiring stories here. Thank you to all of them. I'm honored to share these pages with them and their stories. Special thanks to the handful of heroes I recruited from my own sphere of influence—Ben Fanelli, Craig Cunningham, Dr. Charles Tator, Hilary Knight, and, of course, Kevin Brown—people who have always deeply inspired me, and now I am thrilled their stories may inspire you.

None of this would be possible for me if not for my family at The Sports Network, which gives me the support necessary to do projects like this one, and, of course, my actual family—my wife Cindy and sons Mike and Shawn. Without their love and support, I am nothing.

Finally, to anyone who's reading this book, thank you, thank you, thank you. You made a choice on how to spend your dollars and time, both of which are precious. I hope you enjoy this book as much as I did watching Jim and Sarah do so much of the work.

Take care and all the best.

Jim Lang

In the fall of 2017 I was presented with the idea for a book of first-person stories called *Everyday Hockey Heroes*. Once the concept was explained to me, I just knew I had to be a part of it. Little did I know how much my involvement in the book would change me, and that's because of the people in these pages.

So first, I would like to thank everyone I had the privilege of interviewing for this book. Every single one of the people whom I spoke to had such an incredible story. I ended up learning more about them than I ever thought possible. I thought I knew about the plight of Syrian refugees, the visually impaired, the physically disabled, Canadians of South Asian descent, people with serious brain injuries, the effects of sudden cardiac arrest, first responders with PTSD, racism, sexism, the working class, and women in broadcasting and First Nations people. But after speaking with them, I was shocked how little I really knew. I like to think I became a better and more informed person as I helped them tell their stories. I hope you all felt the same way after reading them.

There are many other people who made this book possible.

Family comes first, and I would like to thank my amazing wife, Patricia, and our daughters, Adriana and Cassandra. I would not have been able to write this book without their patience and understanding.

As always, thanks to my parents for instilling in me the work ethic I needed to complete this task and meet all of the deadlines.

I can never say enough good things about my agent, Brian Wood. He is what they call "a good guy in the room," the kind of guy you want on your team. Thanks, Brian.

Everything about Simon & Schuster Canada is first class. From its publisher, Kevin Hanson, down to its newest employee, Simon & Schuster goes out of its way to help writers. You can't ask for much more than that.

Special thanks to all those at my radio station, 105.9 The Region, for their patience and understanding.

ACKNOWLEDGEMENTS

A number of websites, newspapers, and media organizations were crucial to telling everyone's story. They include NHL.com, ESPN, TSN.ca, Sportsnet.ca, Yahoo! Sports, the *Hockey News*, the *Star*, the *Toronto Sun*, CHL.com, Hockeydb.com, Hockey-reference.com, KeystoneJr.ca, HockeyCanada.ca, blindhockey.com, ryersonian.ca, the *Globe and Mail*, Globalnews.ca, Facebook, allheartfoundation.org, CBC.ca, CTV.ca, and YouTube.

That brings me to my line mates, Bob McKenzie and Sarah St. Pierre.

Our editor, Sarah St. Pierre, was heroic in her passion and dedication in making this book even possible. I simply can't imagine how this book would have been completed without her. She was just that good and just that determined to see it through. So here is a great big stick tap to Sarah for being a real hockey hero.

As a longtime hockey fan, I knew about Bob McKenzie long before I ever met him professionally. His résumé as a reporter, broadcaster, writer, and hockey insider is as good as it gets. So, needless to say, I was thrilled to be able to work alongside him. Not that Bob would be thrilled with my saying that; because true to his hockey roots, Bob is all about the team. Bob's contacts and insight and passion for hockey were major forces in realizing the vision of this book. The bottom line is that Bob McKenzie is a good man who cares about his family, his friends, and the great game of hockey.

As we were in the midst of writing the book I also learned about the power of hockey to bring Canadians together. I remember wiping tears from my eyes when Sheldon Kennedy tried to speak about the Humboldt Broncos bus tragedy on *Hockey Night in Canada*. I also remember Canadians of every conceivable background coming together to help a community in Saskatchewan that most people couldn't find on a map.

From movies to music and to sports, many of us look to famous people or celebrities to be our heroes. In Canada, there are legions of hockey heroes who do great things every day and nobody knows anything about them. I hope this book shines a little of the spotlight on those unsung individuals who overcame any challenge to play, or to be a part of the sport that they love. Because after working on this project, everyone in this book is now a hero to me.

Photography Credits

Wayne with Toronto Aces (*5*): Courtesy of Ann Heron

Wayne's Road Hockey Warriors' fifth year (*8*): Courtesy of Christina Sevcik

Wayne celebrating a goal (*9*): Phil Lameira

Craig on an outdoor rink (*13*): Courtesy of Craig Cunningham

Craig with the Vancouver Giants (*16*): Courtesy of Craig Cunningham

Craig with his mom (*23*): Rachel Huston, SB Nation

Craig with firefighters (*26*): Courtesy of Craig Cunningham

Greg in hockey gear (*31*): Courtesy of Greg Westlake

Greg rollerblading (*32*): Courtesy of Greg Westlake

Greg scoring goal (*38*): Nick Laham/Getty Images

Greg with his mom in 2006 (*39*): Courtesy of Greg Westlake

Mohammed, Ahmad, and Ismael (*51*): Courtesy of Hallie Cotnam

Novice C Coyotes team photo (*55*): Courtesy of Capital Sports Photo

Wayne St. Denis as a kid (*58*): Courtesy of Wayne St. Denis

Wayne St. Denis with the Toronto Ice Owls (*64*): Courtesy of Wayne St. Denis

Harnarayan as a kid (*72*): Courtesy of Harnarayan Singh

The *Hockey Night Punjabi* hosts (*80*): Courtesy of Harnarayan Singh

Harnarayan rinkside (*85*): Courtesy of Harnarayan Singh

Harnarayan with Ron MacLean (*87*): Courtesy of Harnarayan Singh

Andi with roller skates (*90*): Courtesy of Andi Petrillo

Andi in edit suite (*92*): Courtesy of Andi Petrillo

PHOTOGRAPHY CREDITS

Andi with Bobby Orr (*100*): Courtesy of Andi Petrillo

Andi on the *Hockey Night in Canada* set (*104*): Courtesy of Andi Petrillo

Christian as a newborn (*110*): Courtesy of Christian Holmes

Christian and Tie Domi (*112*): Courtesy of Christian Holmes

Ben Fanelli as a kid (*119*): Courtesy of Ben Fanelli

Ben in his silver helmet (*127*): Matthew McCarthy/*The Waterloo Region Record*

Ben at centre ice (*132*): Dan Hamilton/Vantage Point Studios

Dr. Tator at high school (*139*): Courtesy of Marvin Kushner, Forester Yearbook 1953–54

Dr. Tator demonstrating how a spinal cord is damaged (*141*): Tony Bock/Getty Images

Dr. Tator with students (*147*): Courtesy of Dr. Charles Tator

Childhood photo of Hilary (*153*): Courtesy of Hilary Knight

Hilary and her mom at the 2017 world championships (*159*): Courtesy of Hilary Knight

Hilary with her family in Pyeongchang (*164*): Courtesy of Hilary Knight

Selfie of the team (*166*): Courtesy of Hilary Knight

Childhood photo of Brock (*169*): Courtesy of Brock McGillis

Brock in the OHL (*171*): Courtesy of Brock McGillis

Brock training with athletes (*177*): Courtesy of Brock McGillis

Kevin as a kid (*181*): Courtesy of Kevin Monkman

Kevin receiving MVP trophy (*182*): Courtesy of Kevin Monkman

Kevin with the 2017 NAHC gold medal team (*189*): Courtesy of Kevin Monkman

Kevin with Peguis Juniors (*196*): Courtesy of Kevin Monkman

Ray Kline (*200*): Courtesy of Pat Kline

Pat's mom at the 2012 Ray Kline tournament (*206*): Courtesy of Pat Kline

The Halifax Fire Station win (*209*): Courtesy of Pat Kline

Kevin in the fields (*219*): Courtesy of Kevin Brown

Kevin's on-ice injury (*226*): Material republished with express permission of: *Stratford Beacon Herald*, a division of Postmedia Network Inc.

Kevin at *Hockey Day in Canada* puck drop (*233*): Courtesy of Kevin Brown

Call for Stories

Bob McKenzie and Jim Lang want to hear your story for the next book in the series!

Do you have an inspiring story to tell about hockey? Or know a hockey hero who has a story Canadians should hear?

If so, we would love to hear from you for a new book about everyday hockey heroes by Bob McKenzie and Jim Lang. Learn more and tell us your story at www.everydayhockeyheroes.ca.